India

India

By Don Nardo

Enchantment of the World™
Second Series

Children's Press®

An Imprint of Scholastic Inc.

New York Toronto London Auckland Sydney
Mexico City New Delhi Hong Kong
Danbury, Connecticut

Frontispiece: A woman in Rajasthan

Consultant: James Lochtefeld, Professor of Religion and Director of the Asian Studies Program, Carthage College, Kenosha, WI

Please note: All statistics are as up-to-date as possible at the time of publication.

Book production by The Design Lab

Library of Congress Cataloging-in-Publication Data

Nardo, Don, 1947–
   India/by Don Nardo.
       p. cm.—(Enchantment of the world. Second series)
   Includes bibliographical references and index.
   ISBN-13: 978-0-531-25310-6 (lib. bdg.)
   ISBN-10: 0-531-25310-4 (lib. bdg.)
1. India—Juvenile literature. I. Title. II. Series.
   DS407.N315 2012
   954—dc23   2011031118

India

Contents

Cover photo:
A woman serves
traditional Indian
food.

An Indian girl and her mother

Bengal tiger

Land of Striking Contrasts

I NDIA IS A LAND OF TREMENDOUS VARIETY AND STRIKING contrasts. This diversity has existed for thousands of years. About twenty-five hundred years ago, the Greek historian Herodotus wrote the earliest known history text. "There are many tribes of Indians, speaking different languages," he explained. Some "live in the marsh country by the river and eat raw fish." He also described another tribe whose members "will not take life in any form. They sow no seed, and have no houses, and live on a vegetable diet." Herodotus described still more Indian groups that practiced a wide range of other customs.

Opposite: **Some Indians practice age-old rituals. These men are in a temple along the Ganges River.**

Extremes at Every Turn

India is no less diverse today than it was in ancient times. Some areas of the country are quite modern. There, Indians take part in the fast-changing world. But only a few miles from these areas are large regions that are much less developed. One modern traveler to India recalls seeing "billboards advertising cell phones, iPods, and holiday villas and the shiny gas stations with their air-conditioned mini-supermarkets." Yet beyond them, he says, there stretches "an unending vista of rural India," with oxen "plowing the fields in the same manner they have for three thousand years."

Other extremes lurk at every turn in India. Infosys Park, located just outside the large city of Bangalore, is filled with high-tech companies. It is the Indian equivalent of America's Silicon Valley in California. Both places produce innovative computer chips and software—products that are used around the world. The Indians who work in Infosys Park are far better

Thousands of people work at the Infosys campus in Bangalore. Infosys is the second-largest information technology company in India.

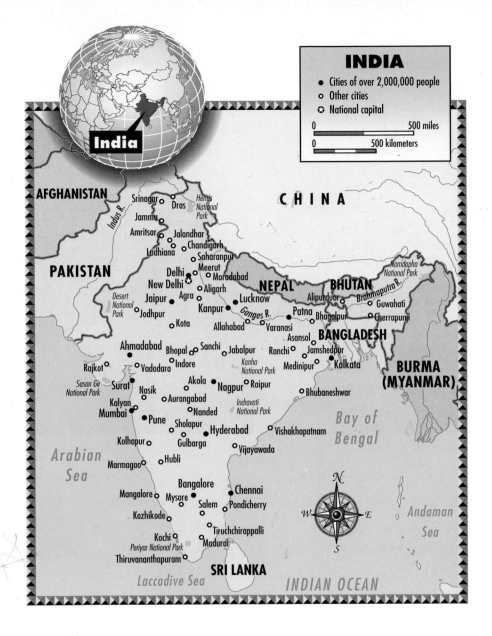

educated than most of their fellow citizens. A whopping 39 percent of the nation's people, including more than half of all Indian women, are illiterate, or unable to read and write. (In comparison, less than 1 percent of people in the United States are illiterate.)

Many wealthy businesspeople in India live in lavish homes.

Some parts of India are very advanced technologically. India possesses nuclear weapons and is a center for information technology. Many homes in India have every modern convenience. But, overall, India's sprawling cities sometimes lack enough clean drinking water and proper sewage facilities. In fact, more than half of the people in India's cities do not have any type of sewage system. Power blackouts are also common in the cities.

Trapped in the Past

Many Westerners who visit India find these sometimes harsh variations in the lives of its people strange and disturbing. A number of writers have tried to explain the existence of such broad extremes within a single country. British journalist Nicki Grihault has come closer than most to capturing the truth. Those eye-opening contrasts can be best understood, she suggests, "by recognizing that India exists in several centuries at the same time. A small, sophisticated modern elite of a few million lives [is] surrounded by hundreds of millions of primitive people."

Looking at India

India is not the only country in the world in which the past and present coexist that way. But such extremes and contrasts

Hundreds of millions of people in India live in poverty.

are sometimes more apparent in India. Partly that's because of its huge population. With 1.2 billion people, it is the world's second most populous nation, trailing only China. Its cities teem with life but strain under their massive populations, unable to provide clean water or deal with all the garbage.

With its huge population, India is also the world's largest democracy. In addition, it is a democratic state lodged between nondemocratic nations in southern Asia. Tensions have long been high in the region, especially between India and neighboring Pakistan, which also has nuclear weapons.

For these reasons, Western and other world leaders keep their eyes on India at all times. As its people strive to modern-

Mumbai is a bustling city. It is the largest city in India and one of the largest in the world.

Hindu women carry pots containing holy water during a procession for peace.

ize their country and lessen the extremes within it, India often teeters on the brink of war. Such a war might force countries around the world to get involved in one way or another. The realities of this potential global threat make studying and understanding India and its enormous diversity more essential now than at any time in its long and eventful history.

People from around the world also look to India as an example of how a nation can function well with extreme diversity. The people of India speak hundreds of different languages. They come from a wide range of ethnic backgrounds. Nearly a billion Indians follow the Hindu religion, more than a hundred million follow Islam, and many millions more are Christian, Sikh, or other religions. India has a belief in tolerance that has allowed this diversity to blossom, creating a remarkably rich culture.

The Great Subcontinent

I NDIA IS AN ENORMOUS COUNTRY. IT COVERS ROUGHLY 1,298,800 square miles (3,364,000 square kilometers), making it the seventh-largest nation on Earth. Spread across this vast expanse is an unusually wide variety of terrains and climates. That variety is more typical of an entire continent than a single nation. So it is not surprising that India is frequently called the Indian subcontinent. India is bordered in the east by Burma (or Myanmar) and Bangladesh; in the northeast by Nepal and Bhutan; in the north by China; and in the west by Pakistan.

Opposite: **The tips of the Western Ghats, a mountain chain that runs along India's western coast, peek above the clouds.**

Building Mountains

India's geographical history has been violent and dramatic. Many millions of years ago, the lands comprising India were part of a much larger early continent located southeast of what is now Asia. Modern scientists call it Gondwanaland.

About 180 million years ago, when dinosaurs ruled the earth, Gondwanaland began breaking up. A massive chunk containing what would turn into India slowly drifted

India's Other Name

The term India comes from the name of one of the nation's largest rivers, the Indus. The nation of India also has a second official name: Bharat. The word *Bharat* comes from Bharata, the name of a legendary Indian leader depicted in this figurine. In many Indian myths, Bharata ruled an empire known as Bharatavarsha, meaning "land of Bharata." Bharata's name also appears within the title of one of India's great national epic poems, the Mahabharata, which means "great story of the Bharatas."

northward. Experts estimate it moved about 8 inches (20 centimeters) each year. That sounds very slow, and indeed it was. But over the course of millions of years, the inches added up to feet and the feet became miles.

Eventually, the great mass of moving land made contact with southern Asia, but it did not stop there. Instead, like a giant freight train, it kept on going, slowly but surely driving itself into and under the larger landmass. As this happened, plains and valleys crumpled, deformed, and thrust upward. About thirty-five million years ago, this slow but steady upheaval raised the Himalayas, the tallest mountain chain in the world.

Today, a large section of the Himalayas stretches across northern India. That mountainous zone is about 1,550 miles (2,500 km) wide and contains more than ninety peaks that tower more than 23,900 feet (7,300 meters) high. South of this giant wall of craggy, desolate mountains lies the main section of the subcontinent. From above, it looks like a big tri-

angle, wider in the north and narrower in the south. Overall, at its widest it is 2,000 miles (3,200 km) from west to east and roughly the same distance from the base of the Himalayas in the north to the southernmost peninsula.

Mount Kanchenjunga, the highest point in India, is the third-highest peak in the world.

India's Geographic Features

Area: 1,298,800 square miles (3,364,000 sq km)

Lowest Elevation: Indian Ocean, sea level

Highest Elevation: Mount Kanchenjunga, 28,201 feet (8,596 m) above sea level

Longest River: Ganges, 1,565 miles (2,519 km)

Largest City (including suburbs): Delhi, population 21,700,000

Average annual rainfall: 47 inches (120 cm)

Largest Glacier: Siachen, 1.7 by 47 miles (2.7 by 75.6 km)

Largest Lake: Chilka (below), about 450 square miles (1,165 sq km) during the wettest season

Largest State: Rajasthan, 132,139 square miles (342,238 sq km)

Smallest State: Goa, 1,429 square miles (3,701 sq km)

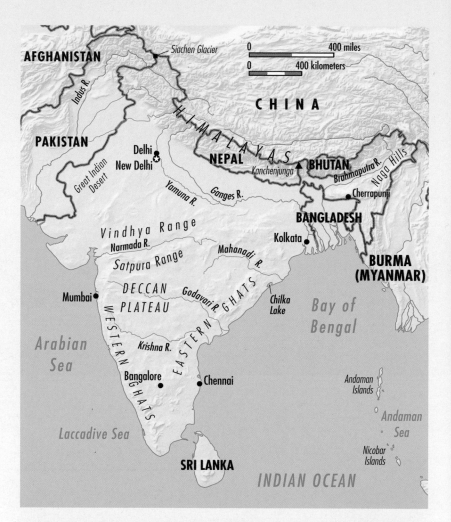

Plain, Plateau, and Coast

The northern and widest portion of India's great triangle is made up mainly of an immense series of remarkably flat river valleys. Stretching some 1,490 miles (2,400 km) from west to east, this vast expanse of well-watered plains contains many rivers. The largest are the Indus, the Ganges, and the Brahmaputra. The plains through which these rivers and their tributaries flow are fertile and green. They were the chief attraction for the many foreign peoples who entered India from the west during ancient and medieval times.

The Indus River cuts across the rugged Ladakh region of northern India.

The Vindhya Mountains separate northern India from southern India.

Some of those settlers or their descendants decided to migrate farther south within the great Indian triangle. As they did so, they came upon a region of rolling hills and then a rugged mountainous area dominated by two mountain ranges—the Vindhyas and the Satpuras. Their southern flanks spread out onto a large upland plateau that makes up much of southern India. Called the Deccan Plateau, most Indians refer to it simply as "the Deccan."

Like the subcontinent itself, the Deccan formed during an episode of extreme geologic violence. About 66 million to 65 million years ago, several enormous volcanic eruptions rocked central India. They spewed out thousands of cubic miles of lava and debris that piled up, creating the great plateau. In some places, it measures up to 400 miles (650 km) from north to south and about 990 miles (1,600 km) from west to east.

The Deccan is arid compared to the northern river valleys. In fact, it gets almost no rain during India's winter months, January and February, or its summer months, March, April, and May. However, the Deccan does get moderate rains off and on during the monsoon seasons, which last from June to December. The monsoons are heavy winds that often carry

Wildflowers brighten the landscape on the Deccan Plateau.

Four Great Indian Cities

On India's western coast lies the enormous city of Mumbai (right), with a population of 19.7 million. It used to be called Bombay, a Portuguese word meaning "good bay." Mumbai is India's main financial center and busiest port. Like many other Indian cities, it features some striking extremes. On the one hand, it has towering skyscrapers, large shopping malls, and rich neighborhoods lined with mini-mansions. On the other, a short walk from these modern wonders leads to huge slums that are home to many of the workers who keep the city running. Mumbai has many notable landmarks, including the Gateway of India. Erected in 1911 on the city's waterfront, this immense arch greets many of the foreign travelers entering India.

On India's eastern coast, along the Bay of Bengal, rests another of the nation's great cities—Kolkata. Its population, counting its suburbs, is about 15.3 million. Until the 1920s, it served as the British colonial capital in India. For that reason, the city boasts many large, stately buildings. A favorite destination for visitors to Kolkata is the Indian Museum. Asia's oldest museum, it features a huge collection of Indian art and cultural artifacts.

Also on the Bay of Bengal, but far to the south of Kolkata, is Chennai, which was once known as Madras. Chennai, which has a population of about 7,400,000, is growing quickly. It has a diverse economy and is an important center of automobile manufacturing, high-tech industries, finance, and health care. Chennai is also a thriving arts center, particularly famous for its classical Indian music and dance performances. Many tourists stop in Chennai to spend time on its long beaches and visit Fort St. George, the first British fortress in India, which dates back to 1639.

One of India's largest and most diverse cities, Bangalore, in the southern state of Karnataka, is also its fastest-growing city. In 2011, the population, including the residents of the city's suburbs, was 7.1 million. Bangalore is often called Asia's Silicon Valley because of its high-tech industries, especially those related to computers. The city has attracted large numbers of educated professionals to run those companies. In turn, members of employees' families attend Bangalore's many high-quality public schools and its several prestigious colleges. It is frequently called the Garden City because of its many well-kept parks. One of those parks, Lal Bagh, features the so-called Glass House, a landmark of modern architecture that attracts thousands of tourists each year.

large rainstorms. Two major monsoons hit India each year. The first, which blows in from the southwest, comes between June and September. The second, with winds from the northeast, arrives between October and December.

Those early Indians who migrated beyond the Deccan found themselves going over the coastal ranges called the Western and Eastern Ghats. From there, they continued downhill to several coastal plains that border the sea.

Warm and Wet

The coastal areas receive plenty of rain, especially during the monsoons. The weather there can be quite hot. The city of Chennai, on the southeastern coast, for instance, has temperatures between 70 and 99 degrees Fahrenheit (21 and 37 degrees Celsius) in the midsummer month of April. Kolkata, Mumbai, and a number of other coastal cities experience similar hot weather. Even in winter, Chennai and most other coastal cities bask in balmy temperatures between 68°F and 84°F (20°C and 29°C).

In contrast, cities in the interior portions of India's great triangle have more variable temperature ranges. The capital, New Delhi, lying in the great river valley plain in the north, has average high temperatures of as much as 103°F (40°C) in the summer. But in the winter months, the thermometer often dips down to 45°F (7°C) at night.

Still farther north, in the Himalayas, 45°F (7°C) is viewed as downright toasty. Most of the year, temperatures in the mountains are well below 32°F (0°C).

Fantastic Variety

FEW COUNTRIES IN THE WORLD CAN BOAST OF HAVING THE tremendous biodiversity that India has. The country is home to more than 47,000 plant species and at least 89,400 animal species. Animals that live in India include bison, rhinoceroses, elephants, and other large mammals. Monkeys swing through trees, and many have made homes in India's cities. Tigers, leopards, and other large cats hunt in its forests and grasslands. Pheasants, geese, pigeons, and hundreds of other kinds of birds soar through its skies. The nation also abounds with snakes, lizards, butterflies, beetles, and thousands of other types of insects.

Tales about India's fantastic variety of living things, some of them found nowhere else on earth, made their way westward to the Middle East and Europe in ancient times. In fact, such stories were one of the factors that gave India the reputation of being an enchanting faraway land. The Greek historian Herodotus believed some fanciful stories about animal life in

Opposite: **More than twenty kinds of monkeys live in India. The Hanuman langur, or northern plains gray langur, is one of the most common.**

India. He seemed convinced of the truth of a tall tale about giant ants that dug for gold. "These creatures," he wrote, "burrow underground [and] throw up the sand in heaps." He added that "the sand has a rich content of gold" and "when the Indians reach the place where the gold is, they fill their bags." Then, Herodotus concluded, the gold collectors run away "as fast as they can go" because the ants can "smell them and at once give chase."

More Precious Than Gold

Although India in fact harbors no gold-digging ants, it does have some animals that Indians view as even more precious than gold. Some residents of southern India revere the water buffalo. And in Buddhism, minor deities called Nagas are shown in the form of cobras, a type of snake.

But no animals are more admired and respected in India than cows. These beasts are seen as holy based on the belief that in the past the gods gave them to humanity as a gift. Indeed, a cow's horns are said to symbolize the divine beings, and the animals' faces represent the sun and moon.

Living Symbols

Living things loom large among India's national symbols. The national animal, the tiger, is a majestic beast that Indians look upon with pride and fascination. Sadly, tigers are threatened with extinction because of hunting and habitat loss. The national bird, the peacock, is no less beautiful or distinctive.

Because of cows' special status in India, no one dares to harm them. The creatures often roam wherever they please, including the crowded cities. It is not unusual to see cows sitting in the street, causing traffic jams, and rummaging through people's garbage. The government has sometimes tried catching them and releasing them in the countryside. But many of those relocated cows eventually end up back in the cities.

Many of the cows foraging in the cities actually belong to people. They return home at night and provide milk to the family. Although cows cannot be harmed, they are valuable after their death. India is one of the world's great leather markets, and the skin can be used after the animal dies.

One-quarter of the world's 1.5 billion cows live in India.

India's cities have played a role in the threat to the lives and survival of the country's wild animals. For more than a century, growing human communities have been encroaching on creatures and their habitats, or living spaces. That has caused the populations of several species to decrease.

Some of India's wild animals are endangered, which means they are threatened with extinction. Among these are large, dangerous snakes such as the Indian python and king cobra; seventy-two bird species, including the Sarus crane, which stands an amazing 6 feet (1.8 m) tall; the elusive swamp deer; and the Asian (or Indian) elephant. Also threatened are a

To Save the Tiger

At the start of the twentieth century, an estimated forty thousand Bengal tigers lived in India. In the following decades, their numbers rapidly declined. This was partly because the British, along with well-to-do Indians, hunted the big cats for sport. Also, poachers, or people who hunt illegally, killed many tigers. The poachers were supplying people around the world with tiger skins for rugs and tiger bones for medicines. In addition, growing human settlements destroyed many tiger habitats. By 1972, only slightly more than eighteen hundred tigers, both in the wild and in captivity, were left in India.

Rising to the challenge, the government initiated Project Tiger in April 1973.

It established twenty-seven tiger preserves, some in national parks and some separate. Together, they cover 14,575 square miles (37,749 sq km). This program helped. By 2010, India's total tiger population had risen to about four thousand.

number of predators, among them the Bengal fox, the Indian wolf, the snow leopard, the tiger, and the Asiatic lion. India is the only country that is home to both lions and tigers.

Fortunately for these animals, the Indian government has stepped in to save them. Over the course of decades, it has

Sarus cranes are the tallest flying birds in the world. Only birds that cannot fly, such as ostriches, emus, and cassowaries, are taller.

Female elephants live in close-knit family groups that include mothers, sisters, aunts, and their offspring.

created some seventy protected national animal parks and about four hundred wildlife sanctuaries. Located all around the country, they provide safe habitats for many endangered species, along with both rare and not-so-rare varieties. Periyar National Park, in the southern Indian state of Kerala, is a

The Lion's Last Stand

By the first years of the twentieth century, the Asiatic lion had been hunted to near extinction in India. No exact figures are known, but experts estimate that fewer than a hundred of these great beasts were left. In the years that followed, their numbers almost certainly continued to shrink. The creation of the Sasan Gir National Park in the western Indian state of Gujarat in 1965 saved the Asiatic lion from extinction. Covering about 545 square miles (1,412 sq km), the park is presently the only existing habitat for the lions, which numbered 411 in 2011. Many other large animals live in Sasan Gir as well, including bears, hyenas, leopards, and antelopes.

good example. Covering 300 square miles (778 sq km), it provides a home for hundreds of kinds of birds and reptiles, along with deer, foxes, bison, and tigers.

Periyar also contains almost a thousand elephants, the largest single wild elephant population in India. Counting those that are captive and domesticated, roughly forty-five thousand elephants are left in India. Asian elephants have smaller ears and are less massive than their African counterparts, though they are still enormous by human standards. Domesticated Indian elephants are used both for transportation and for lifting heavy materials on construction sites. Each animal has a keeper called a mahout, who trains and takes care of it. Usually an elephant and its mahout remain together for life and develop a close bond.

Rice is grown in submerged fields across much of India. It is the staple food in the southern and eastern parts of the country.

India's varied ecosystems support a terrific range of plants. Some of the country's plant species are also found in other parts of Asia or on other continents. The forested foothills of the Himalayas, for instance, contain large stands of pine, cedar, chestnut, apple, birch, and plum trees. Similarly, tens of thousands of farms in the lush northern river valleys grow familiar staple crops such as wheat, rice, and sugarcane. The great plains feature banyan trees, which are found all across southern Asia.

Less widespread trees also abound in India. Groves of Indian rosewood trees, with their small whitish-pink or whitish-yellow flowers, line the banks of rivers. Rosewoods, which provide lumber widely used for furniture and musical instruments, are also found on nearby hillsides up to an elevation of 3,000 feet (900 m). In addition, many hilly slopes are alive with tulip trees, which are typically large and bushy with heart-shaped leaves.

Meanwhile, in the warmer regions, including the coastal plains, sal, or shala, are common. Big broad-leaved trees, these feature leathery leaves and yellow flowers. The resin from the sal is harvested for use in medicines. Aloe vera, a plant common to India's warmer areas, also has wide medicinal use, especially in creams and lotions. It is easily identified by its thick, fleshy, pointed leaves.

About 1,330 of India's plant species are endangered. Among these is the sandalwood tree, found in forested foothills. One of the chief threats to these and other trees comes from the country's poor people. They illegally chop down trees to obtain free firewood or building materials. Because they have no money, they have no other way of obtaining these materials, so they give little thought to the environmental consequences of their actions.

The National Tree

The national tree, the Indian fig tree, or banyan, is an enormous plant that some Indians consider sacred. Its branches spread out horizontally, and large aerial roots fall from the branches to the ground. A single tree can cover many acres. The national flower, the lotus, is also considered sacred, a symbol of beauty, purity, and spirituality.

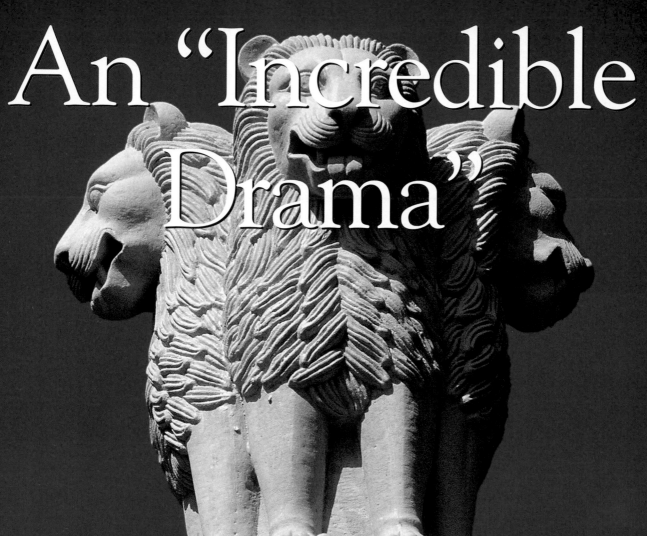

An "Incredible Drama"

INDIA HAS ONE OF THE OLDEST AND MOST COLORFUL histories of any country in the world. "The story of India," noted scholar Michael Wood says, "is a tale of incredible drama." It is a tale filled with "great inventions, enormous diversity, phenomenal creativity, and the very biggest ideas."

India nurtured one of the four so-called cradles of civilization, where complex human culture first emerged. The other three were Mesopotamia (now Iraq), Egypt, and China. All four developed vibrant cultures featuring large-scale agriculture and towns in the 3000s or 2000s BCE.

India's first civilization is sometimes called the Indus Valley civilization or Harappan culture, after Harappa, the first site found. This culture arose between 3000 and 2600 BCE along the banks of the Indus River. (Harappa is now in Pakistan, which was once part of India.) The people of Harappa erected towns and cities. Some covered more than 1 square mile (2.6 sq km) and had up to fifty thousand residents. They lived in well-built brick houses that lined streets laid out in grids. The Harappan people created an empire even bigger than those of ancient Egypt and Mesopotamia.

Opposite: **A lion sculpture that stood atop an ancient pillar of Ashoka is the national emblem of India.**

Game and livestock were crucial to the survival of the early people of India. This vase decorated with a painting of a goat dates back four thousand years.

Rise of the Harappans

It is unknown exactly when the ancestors of the people of Harappa first arrived in India. According to archaeologists, it was sometime between four hundred thousand and two hundred thousand years ago. These early wanderers moved from what are now Afghanistan and Iran eastward into India. They were nomadic hunter-gatherers. Never remaining in one place for very long, they followed their chief food source—migrating herds of antelope and other animals.

Eventually, some of the newcomers settled in the Punjab, in northwestern India. Straddling the region where several smaller rivers flow into the Indus, the Punjab was well watered, supported large numbers of animals, and had extremely fertile soil. Thanks to that soil, by about 4000 BCE, small farms dotted the area. Their owners dwelled in simple huts made of mud bricks, and they used tools and weapons made of stone and animal bones. As time went on, they learned to raise sheep, goats, and cattle.

These early farmers saw the value of cooperation and began building villages. By about 3000 BCE, some of those tiny communities had grown into towns with more than a thousand inhabitants. This marked the birth of Harappan culture, which was both urban and agricultural. Many Harappan towns remained fairly small, with only a few thousand people. But a few developed into full-blown cities with tens of thousands of residents. The largest were Harappa, lying in the midst of

The Harappan people had sophisticated systems for storing water.

the Indus Valley about 580 miles (935 km) inland from the Indian Ocean, and Mohenjo-Daro, roughly 400 miles (640 km) southwest of Harappa.

Evidence shows that Harappa and the other Indus Valley towns were surprisingly advanced for their time. Their layouts were well planned and uniform, with streets meeting at nearly perfect right angles. The fired bricks used to build houses are similar in look and quality to modern ones. Many of those houses were two or three stories high. They featured bathrooms with pottery drainage pipes that carried dirty water out into sewers that ran under the main streets.

The hundreds of Harappan cities and towns, and the farmlands and forests surrounding them, stretched over an area of more than 500,000 square miles (1.3 million sq km). That is

Discovering Harappa

The existence of Harappan civilization was unknown to the modern world until 1856. At that time, India was a British colony, and an amateur British archaeologist named Alexander Cunningham got a tip about some large piles of old bricks near the town of Harappa. He searched the area and discovered many ancient artifacts, including some odd-looking writing carved in stone. Cunningham eventually left to pursue other interests, so the site was more or less forgotten until 1921, when a professional archaeologist, Sir John Marshall, began digging there. He uncovered a large ancient city, which was called Harappa, after the modern town.

The Harappan people made seals that included both writing and pictures of animals, such as bulls. The seals were carved into stone.

almost twice the size of the U.S. state of Texas. Experts are not sure if this great expanse formed a unified empire. But if it did, it was one of the largest of the ancient world.

Unified or not, there is no question that the people of Harappa were ambitious and prosperous. Their merchants sailed in wooden ships to the Persian Gulf and traded with the peoples of ancient Iraq. Small, baked-clay disks made by the Harappan people have been found in the ruins of Mesopotamian cities.

Harappan civilization featured thriving cities.

The Vedic Age

Harappan civilization went into decline after about 1900 BCE. Two centuries later, the larger cities were abandoned. The people who remained lived in small scattered towns that were steadily falling into disrepair. Leading scholars in the early twentieth century advanced a dramatic theory to explain the decline of Harappan culture. They proposed that the people of the Indus Valley were conquered by foreign invaders from somewhere in south-central Asia. These invaders were called the Aryans.

According to the Aryan invasion theory, the intruders attacked the Harappan cities and pushed aside the inhabitants. This seemed to explain how the newcomers managed to set up their own civilization in the area by about 1500 BCE. The period that ensued, lasting from about 1500 to 500 BCE, is known as India's Vedic Age. The word *Vedic* comes from the Vedas, a collection of holy writings revered by the members of the new civilization. The Vedic people established the main religious and social ideas and customs that are the source of later Indian cultures.

There is no question about the reality of Vedic civilization among modern historians. However, most no longer accept the invasion theory. Instead, it is likely that the Aryans simply migrated into India. The Harappan people were probably not conquered, however. It is more likely that most of them migrated away from the central part of the Indus Valley because of changes in the climate, including a long spell of very dry weather. These natural forces caused a long-term decline in agriculture, trade, and, with them, the local economy. The scattered survivors became farmers, like their distant ancestors. Eventually, Vedic culture emerged and spread eastward into the Ganges River valley and beyond.

The principal contribution the Vedic people made to Indian civilization was a collection of major literary works describing their gods, religious beliefs, and myths. These included the Vedas, of which the oldest is the Rig-Veda. The

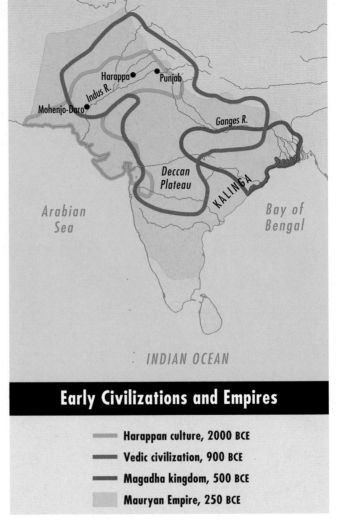

Early Civilizations and Empires

— Harappan culture, 2000 BCE
— Vedic civilization, 900 BCE
— Magadha kingdom, 500 BCE
— Mauryan Empire, 250 BCE

Saraswati is the Vedic goddess of knowledge, art, music, and beauty.

religious beliefs and practices in these Vedas are the foundation for Hinduism, one of India's great religions.

The Vedic texts show that the people who produced them were divided into various tribes, each of which had its own kingdom. The ruler of a kingdom, known as a raja, oversaw a society made up of four main classes. The smallest and most respected of the four was that of the priest-like Brahmins, who were in charge of religious worship and religious learning, which included memorizing the Vedas themselves. There was a warrior class, the Kshatriyas, made up of the rulers, their advisers, and army officers. The Vaishyas were merchants and artisans. Finally, the Sudras were the lowest of the four groups. They worked in service to the members of the upper classes. Over time, these four social classes grew into the caste system that still exists in India.

Invaders from the West

The late Vedic centuries witnessed the growth of villages into towns and towns into bustling cities. At the same time, the many small tribal kingdoms steadily made alliances, forming larger, stronger nation-states. The biggest of these states made war on their neighbors, jockeying for supremacy. By roughly 600 BCE, all of northern India, along with sections of the south, were controlled by sixteen powerful kingdoms. Modern experts call them the Mahajanapadas, meaning "great countries."

The strongest of all these states was Magadha, in northeastern India. By the late 500s BCE, it ruled over most of the Ganges River valley. In these same years, a new religion, Buddhism, appeared in the Ganges region. It did not replace Hinduism. Instead, in the years to come, the two faiths coexisted while Buddhism began to spread beyond India's borders to other parts of southern Asia.

Also in the late 500s BCE, armies from the Persian Achaemenian Empire, centered in southern Iran, invaded western India. Led by their first and greatest king, Cyrus II, the invaders penetrated the Indian kingdom of Gandhara, in the northwestern Punjab. The third Achaemenian king, Darius I, led a considerably larger attack on western India in about 515 BCE. Evidence suggests that he seized control of most of the Punjab lying west of the Indus.

The Achaemenians' grasp on western India did not last long, however. This was because the Achaemenian Empire was overrun in the 330s BCE by the Macedonian Greek conqueror Alexander the Great. In 326 BCE, Alexander led his army across the Indus. Moving to block his advance, Porus, raja of the kingdom of Pauravaa in the Punjab, led his own army forward. At the Jhelum River, which the Greeks called the Hydaspes, the two forces clashed and Alexander won.

Like the earlier invaders, however, Alexander was unable to make much of a dent in the vast and populous India. He had planned to conquer powerful and wealthy Magadha next. But his soldiers, who were exhausted after years of fighting far from home, refused to continue. Alexander therefore departed India. Most of the territory he had seized in the Punjab then fell to an invasion force sent by the king of Magadha.

Rise and Fall of the Mauryans

This move by Magadha was the result of the rise of a new dynasty, or family line of rulers, in that kingdom. Those rulers, the Mauryans, became the most successful that southern Asia had yet seen. In the years that followed, the Mauryan Empire took control of almost all of India.

The Noble Porus

Porus, the raja of the kingdom of Pauravaa, was beaten in a battle with the Macedonian Greek army in 326 BCE. After the battle at the river, Porus met with the victor, Alexander the Great. According to one ancient source, Porus "was a magnificent figure of a man, over seven feet high and of great personal beauty." Alexander was truly impressed and asked, "What do you wish that I should do with you?" Porus replied, "Treat me as a king!" The Greek ruler did exactly that. He restored Porus to his throne, and the two men became friends and allies.

The first important Mauryan ruler was the brash and talented Chandragupta Maurya. Chandragupta conquered northern India in 321 BCE, and his immediate successors pushed southward into the Deccan.

Chandragupta's grandson, Ashoka, came to power in the 260s BCE and became the most important Mauryan king. He invaded the neighboring land of Kalinga, killing at least one hundred thousand people in the process. Then, quite suddenly, he had a change of heart. Appalled by the bloodshed his soldiers had inflicted, Ashoka declared that such mass slaughter was wrong. He converted to Buddhism, which preaches nonviolence, and urged his subjects to strive to be good and kind in their dealings

Thousands of troops under Porus and Alexander fought in 326 BCE. Although Porus's forces had powerful battle elephants, Alexander's forces defeated them.

A Call for Kindness

During the Mauryan Empire, the great leader Ashoka led a bloody invasion of Kalinga but then started preaching peace. After his sudden conversion to non-violence, Ashoka had a message sent out across his land. He had it carved on rocks that were set near the borders and on pillars erected along highways. It said in part, "I am deeply pained by the killing [and] dying [that] take place when an unconquered country is conquered." He went on to denounce war and called for his people to replace violence with "kindness, generosity, truthfulness, purity, gentleness, and goodness."

with others. Hoping to improve the quality of life in his empire, he built hundreds of hospitals, roads, and fountains.

From Guptas to Muslims

Ashoka's successors turned out to be less caring and capable than he had been. They lost the respect of their subjects, and the empire steadily shrank in size and influence. For almost five centuries after the fall of the last Mauryan ruler in 184 BCE, India remained fragmented as many small states struggled for dominance.

This period finally ended in the early 300s CE with the emergence of the Gupta Empire. Its kings brought the states of northern India together and launched a long period of peace and prosperity. The Guptas promoted scientific studies and the arts. Literature, philosophy, mathematics, medicine, and other pursuits thrived so much that later historians viewed the Gupta period as a cultural golden age.

This era did not last. A central Asian people, called the Huns, swept into northern India in the mid-400s. Although they were defeated, a second group of Huns attacked at the end of the same century. They, too, were repulsed. By that time, however, the Gupta Empire was in serious decline. When it disappeared entirely in the 500s, India once again splintered into numerous small states that squabbled among themselves.

Ashoka ordered many Buddhist monuments built, including the Great Stupa at Sanchi in central India.

The disunity of the Indian states in this period left them open to a new wave of outside invaders. The first of a series of Muslim groups arrived in 712. The intruders conquered the southern Punjab and pushed into the Sindh region farther south in what is now Pakistan. Later Muslim assaults on western India took place in the 1000s and 1100s, though these were more often plundering campaigns than attempts to conquer. Finally, in 1206, a permanent Muslim kingdom called the Delhi Sultanate was created in northern India. Powerful and prosperous for more than three centuries, it produced many rulers who championed fine literature, music, art, and architecture.

Art thrived in the Gupta period. This sculpture of the Buddha dates to the fifth century CE.

The Mughals

In 1526, the Delhi Sultanate and some smaller Muslim states that had grown up near it in northern India all fell to a new outside Muslim group. These invaders were known as the Timurids. Under the leadership of Zahir-ud-Din Muhammad

Babur, they established the long-lasting Mughal Empire, one of India's greatest and most accomplished states.

Most Mughals were tolerant of Indian culture, including customs, artistic styles, and the Hindu religion, which a majority of Indians followed. Several Mughal rulers embraced architecture that combined Indian, Islamic, and other styles. Perhaps the most renowned examples of this cultural fusion is the Taj Mahal, in Agra, in north-central India. Completed in 1643, it was erected by Babur's great-great-grandson, Shah Jahan. The imposing structure brings touches of Indian, Iranian, and Islamic architecture together in a unique way.

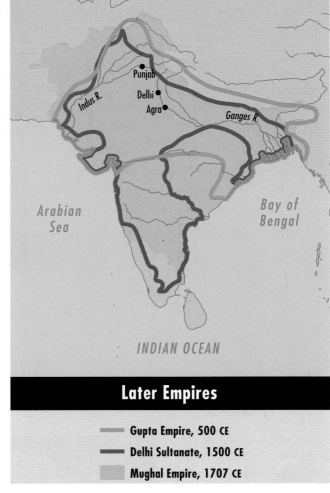

Later Empires

— Gupta Empire, 500 CE
— Delhi Sultanate, 1500 CE
Mughal Empire, 1707 CE

The Jewel in the Crown

The Mughal Empire eventually fell into decline. By the early 1700s, several smaller kingdoms vied for control of the northern river valleys, the Deccan, and other regions. Watching these quarrels were Europeans who had recently set up trading posts in India. In particular, the British East India Company viewed India as a vast untapped market. This influential company steadily expanded its interests, moving into one Indian region and market after another. As it did, it started hiring soldiers,

Empire Builder

Zahir-ud-Din Muhammad Babur, the founder of the Mughal Empire, was born in 1483. He was descended from the great Mongolian ruler Genghis Khan. In addition to his talents as a military and political leader, Babur was known for his physical strength and his interest in history. He sometimes took groups of his men on hunting parties. He filled what little spare time he had with a personal love—gardening.

both for protection and to enforce its will. The officers were Europeans; the regular troops were native Indians called sepoys.

As the company's power in India increased, the authority and influence of the Mughals and other Indian rulers decreased. This caused many Indians to fear and despise the British pres-

The Mughal leader Shah Jahan was a major supporter of the arts. Many outstanding monuments were built during his rule, and he is said to have established 777 gardens in Kashmir, in northern India.

ence in the region. Tensions rose for several decades until a large rebellion, sometimes called the Sepoy Mutiny, erupted in 1857. Britain sent troops to reinforce the company's paid forces, and the combined foreign army crushed the native rebels. The British government then dissolved the British East India Company and imposed direct rule over most of India.

Britain's colonial rule of India came to be called the British Raj. The British had many other colonies across the globe at that time. Of these, India was easily the most profitable. It earned the nickname the Jewel in the Crown, in reference to the crown worn by the British queen. Not surprisingly, Britain did not want to part with such a valuable asset.

Independence

The British held tight to India for many reasons, including arrogance. The general attitude was that the Indians, along

The Taj Mahal

The Mughal ruler Shah Jahan built the Taj Mahal as a tomb for his wife, Mumtaz, who died in 1631. Some twenty thousand workers toiled for twelve years to raise the monument. The huge central structure, in which the royal couple's remains rest, is topped by a dome 144 feet (44 m) across. Outside the main building, a wide tiled terrace is marked off at the corners by four towers, each rising 131 feet (40 m). Beyond the terrace stretch magnificent gardens and a pool that perfectly reflects the image of the Taj Mahal for visitors standing in the right spot.

with most other non-Western peoples, were inferior and incapable of self-rule. One high-ranking Briton in India summed up that view, saying, "Chaos would prevail in India if we were ever so foolish to leave the natives to run their own show. Ye gods! [The Indians] are still infants as regards governing, [and] their so-called leaders are the worst of the lot."

In the face of British resistance to change, a strong yearning for self-rule grew among the Indians. In 1885, a group of Indians and Britons founded the Indian National Congress, or INC. Its chief goal was to seek workable, and hopefully peaceful, ways to bring about India's independence.

British ships were common in the waters off India when the British East India Company controlled the region. Here, a British ship approaches Mumbai.

The INC made little progress at first. However, its efforts began to gain steam in the 1920s, thanks to a smart and courageous Indian thinker and political activist named Mohandas Gandhi. He led a series of nonviolent protests and helped to coordinate large-scale boycotts of British goods. The British authorities tried to stifle the protests, but it was no use. Gandhi's shrewd approach was eventually successful, and in 1946 Britain agreed to grant India independence.

British soldiers attack Delhi during the Sepoy Mutiny. The rebellion was led by sepoys, Indian soldiers who had been working for the British.

National Hero

Mohandas Gandhi (center) never served as president or prime minister, but he was the most revered Indian national leader of the modern era. He was born on October 2, 1869, in western India. As a young man, Gandhi journeyed to Britain to study law and then to South Africa. Many Indians lived there, and he tried to fight discrimination against them by local whites.

Returning to India in 1914, Gandhi set a new goal: to help his country gain independence from Britain. His main tactic was nonviolent protest. He called it *satyagraha*, which in his native language, Gujarati, means "the force of truth" or literally "holding on to truth." This approach landed Gandhi and many of his followers in jail. Yet he assured his followers that their suffering would slowly but surely focus worldwide attention on the plight of the Indian people. In 1942,

he said that nonviolent protest "does not mean meek submission to the will of the evil-doer, but it means the pitting of one's whole soul against the will of the tyrant. Working under this law of our being, it is possible for a single individual to defy the whole might of an unjust empire to save his honor, his religion, his soul, and lay the foundation for that empire's fall."

Eventually, Gandhi's remarkable courage, great wisdom, relentless hard work, and personal sacrifice paid off. India gained independence in 1947. Just months later, on January 30, 1948, the seventy-eight-year-old national hero was shot to death in Delhi by a young Indian man who thought Gandhi was being too nice to Pakistan. Millions of people wept openly as the country mourned the passing of the most beloved public figure it had ever known.

That much-desired freedom came at a heavy price, however. As the end of the Raj approached, many Indian Muslims became worried. They formed a minority in a population made up primarily of Hindus. Concerned that the Hindus might oppress Muslims, Muslim leaders demanded that the new India be partitioned, or divided, into two separate nations. In August 1947, two new countries were established: independent India, which was home to people of many different religions, and Pakistan, populated mainly by Muslims.

Although most Indians were glad to be free of the Raj, the influence of the British remained strong. In setting up their

Leading figures in the Indian independence movement included Mohandas Gandhi (left), a political activist and religious leader, and Jawaharlal Nehru (center), who would become India's first prime minister.

Indian and British officials met in 1947 to discuss the plan for India's independence.

new government, for example, the Indians chose a democracy similar in many respects to that of Britain. Also, the two nations became close allies and trading partners.

The Unbroken Chain

In the decades that followed, India attempted to modernize itself. A succession of dynamic leaders headed these efforts. The most popular and successful were India's first prime minister, Jawaharlal Nehru; his daughter, Indira Gandhi; and her son, Rajiv Gandhi.

One of the nation's major achievements was feeding millions of hungry people. In the 1950s, India suffered from severe food shortages, but by the 1990s it was producing food surpluses. There were other advances put into place in the

Emergence of Bangladesh

When Pakistan was created in 1947, it consisted of two sections. West Pakistan was made up of the lands surrounding the Indus Valley. East Pakistan was located north of the Bay of Bengal on the other side of India. This situation changed in 1971 when East Pakistan became the independent country of Bangladesh.

second half of the twentieth century. Thousands of new factories, roads, dams, canals, power plants, and schools were built. High-tech industries, especially computer-related information technology and software development, grew in India. During this period, civil rights for women also expanded.

In 1974, India announced that it had nuclear weapons. Many Indians, both inside and outside the government, felt

Indira Gandhi speaks at a rally in 1969. She served as India's prime minister from 1966 to 1977 and from 1980 to 1984.

this was necessary to make the nation safe against aggression by its neighbors. They especially worried about Pakistan. The two countries distrusted each other from the start and fought four short but bloody wars (in 1947, 1965, 1971, and 1999), mostly over disputed territory.

Thus, a combination of sweeping internal reforms and ongoing tensions on the borders thrust India into the modern world in only a few decades. Dealing with today's realities,

Workers lay telecommunications cables in a tunnel in New Delhi.

however, has not caused India's people to lose touch with their long and eventful past. They retain many of the beliefs and customs of their ancestors. Nehru captured the unique blend of past and present that endures in India when, shortly before his death, he said, "I have discarded much of the past tradition and customs, and am anxious that India should rid herself of all shackles that bind [and] divide her people. [Yet] I am conscious that I too, like all of us, am a link in that unbroken chain which goes back to the dawn of history in the immemorial past of India."

Indian soldiers fire weapons along the border with Pakistan in 1999.

An "Incredible Drama" **61**

The World's Largest Democracy

WITH A POPULATION OF 1.2 BILLION PEOPLE, INDIA is the world's largest democracy. When it gained independence from Great Britain in 1947, its leaders worked in a group called the Constituent Assembly to put together a constitution. That document, which went into effect on January 26, 1950, provided a basic framework for the country's government.

In some ways, that government is quite similar to the British political system. Like Britain, India has a parliamentary democracy. In such a system, the executives who run the government are called ministers. They are chosen by the members of the national legislature, who themselves are directly elected by the people. India's chief legislature, the House of the People, is modeled on Britain's House of Commons.

But India also has a federal system that resembles the one in the United States. In both countries, the national, or federal, government shares power with state governments. Also

Opposite: **Soldiers march in a parade on Republic Day, which celebrates the day the Indian Constitution went into effect.**

The Indian Tricolor

The great Indian leader Mohandas Gandhi declared, "A flag is a necessity for all nations. Millions have died for it. It will be necessary for [all Indians] to recognize a common flag to live and to die for." India's national flag, known as the Tricolor, was designed by Pingali Venkayya and officially adopted by the government on July 22, 1947. The flag has three horizontal stripes. The top one, colored saffron, or orange-tan, symbolizes the nation's courage. The middle stripe is white. Imprinted at its center is the circular Ashoka Chakra, an early Buddhist sign standing for truth and peaceful change. The flag's bottom stripe is green and represents the great fertility of India's soil.

in both countries, the federal government is stronger than and usually overshadows the state governments.

The Chief Executives

Like the U.S. system, India's government is divided into three main branches. The executive branch includes the officials who run the country. Members of the legislative branch make the laws and choose the executives. The judicial branch consists of the judges who oversee the courts.

The executive branch of India's government has two chief officials—a president and a prime minister. This is sometimes confusing to people in the United States who are used to having a single executive, the president. The Indian system is easily understood, however, when one realizes that the presidency is mostly a ceremonial office. One prominent Indian politician summed it up well. The president "represents the nation," he said, "but does not rule the nation." It is the prime minister who actually holds the executive power and runs the country.

The president is elected to a five-year term of office by the members of the national legislature and the members of the state legislatures. In all, these bodies contain roughly forty-five hundred people at any given moment. (The legislators also elect a vice president who serves if the president dies or is otherwise unable to continue in office.) Once in office,

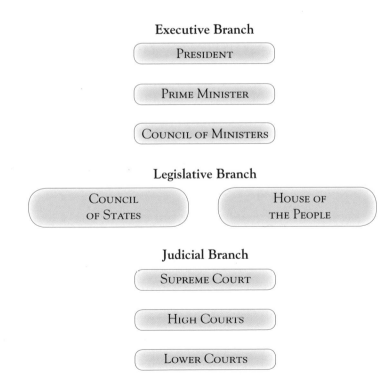

NATIONAL GOVERNMENT OF INDIA

Executive Branch

PRESIDENT

PRIME MINISTER

COUNCIL OF MINISTERS

Legislative Branch

COUNCIL OF STATES

HOUSE OF THE PEOPLE

Judicial Branch

SUPREME COURT

HIGH COURTS

LOWER COURTS

Manmohan Singh became the prime minister of India in 2004. A follower of the Sikh religion, he is the first non-Hindu to be prime minister.

the president appoints a prime minister. By both custom and law, the prime minister is the leader of the political party that holds the majority of seats in the House of the People. So usually the president has no real choice, and the appointment of the prime minister is a formality. The only exception is when no party holds a majority of seats in the House of the People. Then the president invites the largest party to try to form a majority.

The president appoints the members of the Council of Ministers. This small group of officials works closely with the prime minister to run the country on a daily basis. Because the prime minister advises the president on who should be in the council, once again the president's choices are ceremonial.

Finally, the president appoints the governors of India's states and territories as well as the judges of the supreme and high courts. He does this with the advice and instructions of the prime minister and members of the council.

Together, the president, vice president, prime minister, and members of the council make up the country's executive branch. Of all these officials, the prime minister is the most powerful. He or she oversees the various government agencies, makes important national policy decisions, schedules sessions of the legislature, and meets with the heads of state of foreign nations.

The Indian Parliament

The national legislature that works closely with India's prime minister is called Parliament. Like Britain's Parliament and the U.S. Congress, it is divided into two houses. The upper house is the Rajya Sabha, or Council of States. Of its roughly 250 members (the exact number varies slightly), 12 are appointed

The Tireless Nehru

One of India's greatest modern leaders, Jawaharlal Nehru was born on November 14, 1889, in northern India. He first went to school locally but later studied in Britain, where he earned his law degree. Soon afterward he joined Gandhi's Indian National Congress, which was devoted to gaining independence from British rule. In 1929, Nehru became the organization's president. When independence finally came in the 1940s, he was chosen to be the country's first prime minister. A tireless, caring public official, he was a big promoter of democracy and the unity of all Indians. Nehru died on May 27, 1964, in Delhi.

India's Sprawling Capital

Over the centuries, a major town grew up and eventually served as the capital of a succession of kingdoms and empires.

A major turning point for the city came in 1947 when India gained its independence. Large numbers of people native to the western Punjab did not want to live in the newly formed Pakistan. So they streamed into Delhi, swelling its population. Today, with almost twenty-two million people (counting those in the suburbs), it is one of the largest cities in the world. It is also one of the most ethnically diverse cities because people from all across India have moved there.

The sprawling city is divided into several sections, each with a distinct look. Old Delhi contains many stately monuments from the Mughal period (the 1500s

The capital of India is New Delhi. It sits in northern India, right next to a larger city called Delhi. The region of northern India where the capital now rests was first inhabited sometime in the second millennium BCE, more than three thousand years ago. At some point, bands of nomadic hunters settled there and became farmers.

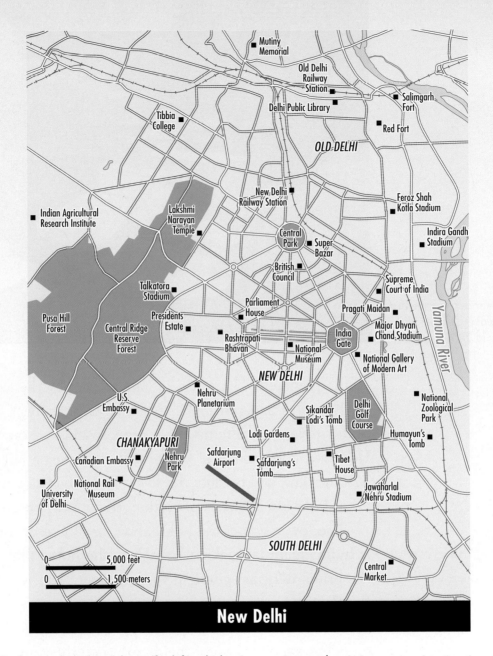

New Delhi

and 1600s). These include the Red Fort (far left), which was built to be the residence of the Mughal emperors. New Delhi features wide streets and large mansions built by the British. All around the city are middle-class suburbs, and beyond lie large poverty-stricken slums.

Among the city's many tourist attractions is Jaipur House. In the 1700s, local royalty lived there. Now it is home to the National Gallery of Modern Art, which displays works by early modern and present-day Indian and British artists.

Meira Kumar became the first female speaker (leader) of the Lok Sabha in 2009.

by the president. The other 238 are elected by the legislatures of the states and territories. All members of the Council of States serve six-year terms. They propose and vote on new laws. However, both houses of Parliament must pass a bill before it becomes law, and because the lower house has more members, it has more say in government than the upper house.

The lower house, the Lok Sabha, or House of the People, is India's main lawmaking body. It is the house that produces the prime minister, giving it further clout. The House of the People also has authority over how the country spends money. The House of the People has a maximum of 552 members. The president appoints two of them, and the others are elected by the people of India's states and territories. These terms are for a maximum of five years. In some cases, the terms are shorter. This can happen if no party has a ruling majority. It can also happen if the ruling party requests that elections be held early.

The Courts

India's judicial branch of government has three levels. At the lowest level are the lower courts. Above them are the high courts, and at the top level is the Supreme Court. The lower courts exist all across the country. Within a state, each local district, called a *zilla*, has two judges. One tries criminal cases, and the other oversees civil cases, which are those that do not involve crimes. Lower court judges are appointed by the state governors.

The High Court of Bombay is one of eighteen high courts in India.

The National Anthem

India's national anthem, "*Jana Gana Mana*," consists of the first verse of a song written by the Indian poet Rabindranath Tagore. It was adopted in 1950.

Hindi lyrics:

Jana-gana-mana-adhinayaka, jaya he
Bharata-bhagya-vidhata.
Punjab-Sindh-Gujarat-Maratha
Dravida-Utkala-Banga
Vindhya-Himachala-Yamuna-Ganga
Uchchala-Jaladhi-taranga.
Tava shubha name jage,
Tava shubha asisa mage,
Gahe tava jaya gatha,
Jana-gana-mangala-dayaka jaya he
Bharata-bhagya-vidhata.
Jaya he, jaya he, jaya he,
Jaya jaya jaya, jaya he!

English translation:

You are the ruler of the minds of all people,
Dispenser of India's destiny.
Your name rouses the hearts of
Punjab, Sind, Gujarat, and Maratha,
Of the Dravida and Orissa and Bengal;
It echoes in the hills of the Vindhyas and Himalayas,
Mingles in the music of Jamuna and Ganges and is
Chanted by the waves of the Indian Sea.
They pray for your blessings and sing your praise.
The saving of all people waits in your hand,
You dispenser of India's destiny.
Victory, victory, victory to you!

If a lower court judge cannot resolve a dispute, the case goes up to the high courts. There are eighteen high courts in the country. In addition to resolving arguments raised in the lower courts, the high courts supervise and advise the lower court judges.

The chief justice is the leader of up to twenty-six judges who serve on the nation's highest court, the Supreme Court. Those judges are chosen by the president on the advice of the prime minister. They remain on the job until they are sixty-five. The judges of India's Supreme Court supervise the high courts and resolve legal disputes raised in cases heard in those courts. Also, like the U.S. Supreme Court, the Indian court can decide if a law is constitutional.

State Governments

India is divided up into twenty-eight states and seven union territories. Each state has an executive branch of government that includes a governor, whose job is much like that of the president. The state executive branch also includes a chief minister and a council of ministers. Administrators appointed by the Indian president govern the union territories. The legislative branch of each state consists of an elected legislative assembly. Some states also have a second legislative body, called the legislative council.

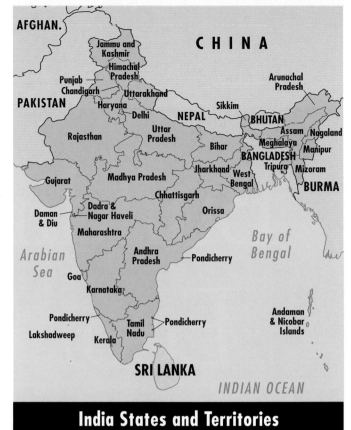

India States and Territories

Ministers from the state of Assam pose after taking the oath of office in 2011.

Building an Economy

I NDIA HAD THE FIFTH-LARGEST NATIONAL ECONOMY in the world in 2010. (The four larger ones were those of the European Union, the United States, China, and Japan.) India's economic success is extraordinary considering how much the country has progressed in only a few decades. Before gaining independence in 1947, Indians were not allowed to produce most of the goods they used. Indians supplied raw materials to the British, who used them to manufacture goods in their own country. Britain then sold those goods to India for a profit.

As a result, India lacked a major manufacturing base of its own. It did have many small farmers, but they were mostly poor and used outdated equipment and methods. So they were unable to produce enough food to sustain the nation's growing population.

In 1947, therefore, India faced the daunting task of building a world-class economy almost from scratch. It took time, but

Opposite: **A worker removes fabric from a drying line at a manufacturing plant.**

since 1997 India's economy has grown by an impressive 7 percent each year. Moreover, many experts predict it will have the world's third-largest economy by 2030 and the largest by 2050.

An Economic Snapshot

Although India has the world's fifth-largest economy, it has the globe's second-largest population. Thus, the economic pie must be divided among a large number of people. The income of the average Indian worker remains low by U.S. and European standards. Although there are 153,000 millionaires in India, most Indians are lower middle class or poor. According to the World Bank, 37 percent of the population, or 410 million people, lived below the poverty line in 2008. Still, the situation is improving, and the percentage of poor people in India is declining.

Indian Currency

The main unit of India's currency is the rupee. In 2011, 46 rupees equaled US$1.00, and 1 rupee was equal to about US$0.02. In paper money, rupees come in values of 1, 2, 5, 10, 20, 50, 100, 500, and 1,000. A portrait of the patriot and political activist Mohandas Gandhi appears on the front of all denominations of Indian paper money. The backs vary, however. The back of the 10-rupee note shows a tiger, an elephant, and a rhinoceros, while the 100-rupee note has an image of the Himalayas. Indian coins commonly come in values of 1, 2, 5, and 10 rupees.

An Indian's Purchasing Power

Purchasing power is the amount of goods or services that can be purchased with a unit of currency. In 2010, the purchasing power (in American dollars) of an average Indian worker was about $3,500 per year. In comparison, the yearly purchasing power of an average American worker was $47,200 and that of a British worker was $34,800.

A high proportion of Indians—just over 50 percent of the labor force in 2011—work in agriculture. Overall, modern Indian farmers are doing much better than their parents and grandparents did. On average, however, farmers make less than factory workers or people who work in services, which include everything from health care to restaurant work to computer programming.

An Indian farmer plows a wet rice field. About half of India's people work in agriculture.

Workers take part in a training session at Infosys. The company employs more than 130,000 people in India.

Workers in the fastest-growing service industry, information technology, command higher salaries because the work they do is worth more in the marketplace. About 34 percent of Indians work in service-oriented jobs. They create 55 percent of the country's economic output. In contrast, farmers make up more than half of the workforce but generate only 16 percent of India's total economic production.

Expanding Agriculture

India's agricultural sector is vital to the welfare of the country and its people. It has come a long way in only a few decades. Following independence, Indian farmers were at first unable to feed everyone in the country, and some food had to be imported. Over time, however, major advances occurred. The first was the so-called Green Revolution of the 1970s, when the government helped begin cultivating several million acres

What India Grows, Makes, and Mines

Agriculture

Rice	79.6 million metric tons
Wheat	74.6 million metric tons
Millet and other coarse grains	27.8 million metric tons

Manufacturing (value in U.S. dollars)

Jewelry	$28,460,000,000
Refined fuels and oils	$28,440,000,000
Electrical machinery and equipment	$9,540,000,000

Mining

Coal	537,000,000 metric tons
Iron ore	212,613,000 metric tons
Bauxite	13,363,000 metric tons

India produces about 20 percent of all the rice grown in the world.

of unused land. It also funded better irrigation equipment, higher-quality seeds, and other improvements.

These efforts were successful. Food production in India has increased nearly every year since 2000. By 2009 an estimated 109 million tons (99 million metric tons) of the chief food crop, rice, were grown. That made India the second-largest producer of rice in the world.

In addition to rice, Indian farmers grow wheat, and the country is second in global wheat production. They also grow coarse grains like millet as well as oilseed, cotton, sugarcane, lentils, potatoes, and tea. India is the world's biggest grower and consumer of tea.

Manufacturing and Mining

Industry, which accounts for about 29 percent of India's economic output, consists of thousands of factories and mining operations. The largest single manufacturing sector is the textile industry. Its roughly twenty million workers are employed in more than eleven hundred factories and generate one-fifth of all Indian-made products.

India also manufactures steel, cement, chemicals, transportation and electrical equipment, cars, refined fuels and other petroleum products, medicines, jewelry, and computer software. In addition, it is the world's biggest producer of rubber. These products are used by Indians and exported to other countries.

Many of the raw materials used to manufacture the thousands of goods made in India come from its huge mining industry. These materials range from marble, manganese, coal, bauxite, and other minerals to iron, copper, gold, lead, and other metals. India is the world's third-largest producer of manganese and coal and ranks fourth in iron ore and marble.

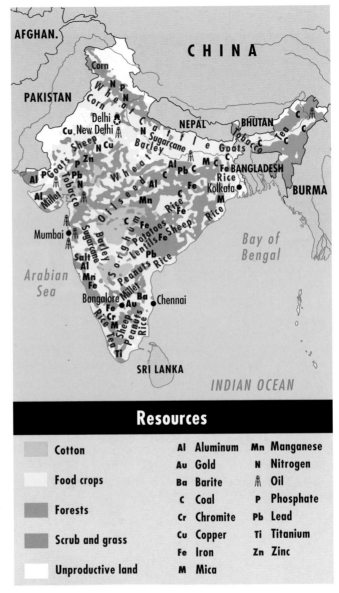

India's mining and manufacturing operations are expanding each year. Overall, Indian industry grew by a whopping 19.4 percent from April 2009 to April 2010.

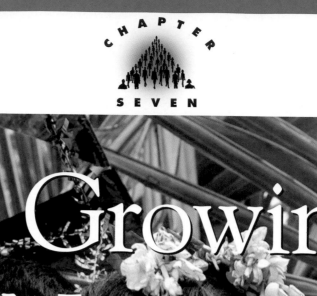

A Growing Nation

INDIA'S POPULATION IS GROWING QUICKLY. IN 1991, the country had about 846 million residents. By 2001, a mere decade later, that figure had risen to just over a billion, and in 2011 it reached 1.2 billion. That total is second only to China, which has slightly more than 1.3 billion people. Presently, India's population is expanding at a rate of 3 percent annually. Experts predict that the country will become the world's most populated nation by 2050.

The distribution of India's people is also changing. Until early modern times, the vast majority of Indians were farmers dwelling in the countryside. As late as 1901, only 11 percent of India's people lived in cities and towns. This was why the great Indian leader Mohandas Gandhi, who was then a young man, famously said that India's soul could be found in its villages.

In the twentieth century, however, rural people started migrating into the cities in large numbers. Their reasons varied. Most often they were searching for jobs or other

Opposite: **About 30 percent of Indians are under the age of fifteen.**

Populations of Major Cities (with suburbs, 2011 est.)

Delhi	21,700,000
Mumbai	19,700,000
Kolkata	15,300,000
Chennai	7,400,000
Bangalore	7,100,000

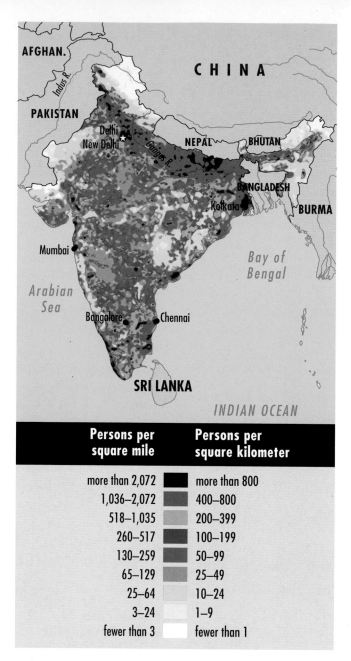

Persons per square mile	Persons per square kilometer
more than 2,072	more than 800
1,036–2,072	400–800
518–1,035	200–399
260–517	100–199
130–259	50–99
65–129	25–49
25–64	10–24
3–24	1–9
fewer than 3	fewer than 1

opportunities they perceived as lacking in the countryside. Today, around 340 million people, almost a third of the population, live in cities. This is approximately equivalent to India's entire population in 1947, when it gained independence from Britain.

Great Diversity

In addition to its large size and ongoing rapid growth, India's population is extremely diverse. People speak many languages and come from many different ethnic backgrounds. The Indian government does not officially identify separate ethnic and racial groups within the country except for some small indigenous groups.

This is because India's ethnic diversity is complex. The complexity is partly the result of a steady influx of settlers from other lands over the course of many centuries. These immigrants sometimes lived among and married India's original inhabitants. Among these outside groups were Greeks, Jews, Iranians, Portuguese (called Goans), Africans (called Siddhis), British (called Anglo-Indians), and other Europeans.

Members of these various groups mixed with only a small portion of the country's original inhabitants, however. So the ethnicity of most Indians has not changed much over the centuries. Studies done on ancient Harappan skeletons show that they closely resembled modern Indians. Scientists have found no marked genetic differences between ancient Indians and modern Indians. "If you could get into a time machine and visit northern India 10,000 years ago," scientist Peter Underhill says, "you'd see people [who are] similar to the people there today."

The state of Goa, on the west coast, was long ruled by Portugal, a Catholic country. Many Goans, such as these people attending a celebration at a church in Siolim, remain Catholic.

That said, India is a large country, and people from different parts of the country often look different. People from Bengal, in eastern India, look different than people from southern India. People from the northeast typically look more like central Asians.

A girl and her mother ride a train in Bengal.

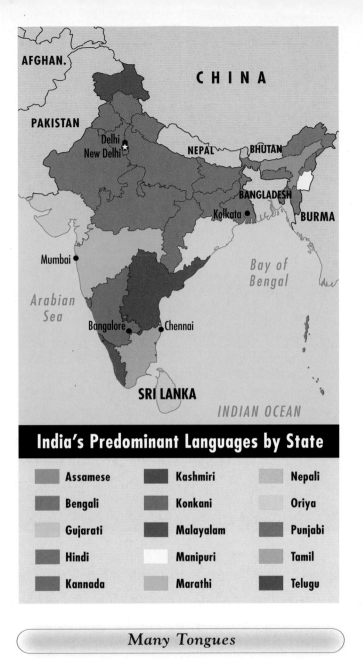

India's Predominant Languages by State

Assamese	Kashmiri	Nepali
Bengali	Konkani	Oriya
Gujarati	Malayalam	Punjabi
Hindi	Manipuri	Tamil
Kannada	Marathi	Telugu

Many Tongues

The outside groups that entered India spoke a wide range of languages. In addition, some of the country's original languages changed over time. The result is that the Indian subcontinent is home to many separate tongues. Fourteen major languages are spoken, along with some three hundred minor ones.

कार्यालय
वन क्षेत्र पदाधिकारी
गारु
डालटनगंज दक्षिणीवन प्रमंडल

चोर शिकारियो
को रोकिये

Signs written in Hindi warn against illegal hunting. Hundreds of languages are spoken in India, but Hindi is the most common.

The oldest major language in India is Sanskrit. The Vedas and other early Hindu texts were written in Sanskrit. It is widely viewed as a classical, treasured language in the same way that Latin and Greek are in Europe. Though ancient, Sanskrit is not a dead language. It is still employed in Hindu rituals and hymns and studied in schools. Also, some literature and music lyrics continue to use Sanskrit.

Of India's widely spoken modern tongues, the main one is Hindi, which is also the country's official language. Spoken by close to five hundred million people, it is understood in most parts of India, particularly in the north. Hindi is closely related to another Indian language called Urdu.

Although many people in southern India understand Hindi, more common are languages from the Dravidian language family. These include Tamil, Telugu, Kannada, and Malayalam.

The Indian government recognizes English as a secondary official language for administrative purposes. Initially introduced by the British, its total number of speakers in India is unknown. Most well-educated Indians speak English, and more than half the people in southern India speak it.

Many languages in India, including Hindi and Sanskrit, are written in a script called Devanagari. It uses curved strokes with a solid line across the top. Other languages in India use scripts specific to that language. For example, the Gujarati language uses the Gujarati alphabet. It looks similar to Devanagari, but does not have a solid line connecting the letters.

India's Leading Languages	
Hindi	41%
Bengali	8%
Telugu	7%
Marathi	7%
Tamil	6%
Urdu	5%

Common Hindi Words and Phrases

haan	yes
na	no
dhanyavad	thank you
kripaya	please
kshama karen	excuse me/sorry
namasté	hello/good-bye
Aap kaisé hain?	How are you?
Mera naam…	My name is…

Many Faiths

F EW COUNTRIES ARE AS RELIGIOUSLY DIVERSE AS INDIA. In fact, four of the world's major religions—Hinduism, Buddhism, Sikhism, and Jainism—began there. Many other faiths entered the subcontinent over the centuries, among them Islam, Christianity, Judaism, and Zoroastrianism. India's democratic constitution guarantees freedom of religion, so dozens of different faiths coexist and are practiced with great zeal throughout India.

Hinduism

The most widely practiced religion in India is Hinduism. More than 80 percent of the people are Hindus. Hinduism was born out of beliefs and rituals of the Vedic people. The original Vedic faith changed over the centuries. Worshippers added new concepts, rituals, and gods until the version now called Hinduism emerged.

As the Vedic religion turned into Hinduism, new deities were embraced. But older gods were not entirely rejected. As a result, Hindus came to accept the existence of many gods. Among the

Religions in India	
Hinduism	81%
Islam	13%
Christianity	2%
Sikhism	2%
Buddhism	1%
Jainism	0.5%

The Hindu god Indra is sometimes shown riding his elephant Airavata.

earliest was Dyaus, a sky god who controlled the weather and created thunder and lightning. Over time, he became less important than his divine son, Varuna, seen as a wise figure who oversaw both the heavens and the underworld. Another of Dyaus's sons, Indra, became the Hindu god of the heavens, war, and rain.

A Hymn to Indra

Many Hindu gods appear in one of India's earliest and most revered ancient religious texts, the Rig-Veda. This Vedic verse praises Indra.

O Hero, Lord of Bounties, praised in hymns, may power and
*   joyfulness be his who sings [praises] to you.*
Lord of a Hundred Powers, stand up to lend us succor [aid] in this
*   fight....*
In every need, in every fray [fight], we call as friends [on]
*   Indra, the mightiest of all.*
If he will hear us, let him come with succor of a thousand kinds,
*   and all that strengthens [us], to our call.*

Brahma was a principal creator-god. Other Hindu gods include Vishnu, who is said to manage the universe, and Shiva, the destroyer deity. Each of these gods can assume alternate forms. The most familiar example is Vishnu. In Hindu lore, he came to earth as the heroes Rama and Krishna. Each of these forms is the same god. They just appear different depending on the perspective from which one views them.

Shiva is often depicted performing a powerful, violent dance called the Tandava.

Another important aspect of Hinduism is the belief in reincarnation. It holds that the soul is immortal and after death comes back to life in a different body. This process supposedly occurs over and over again, as the soul continually tries to become one with the universal spirit. Hindus believe that the success one achieves in a given lifetime depends on karma. A sort of law of moral costs, karma ensures that good behavior will be rewarded and bad behavior will be punished. Karma can act in this life or in the next. As one scholar puts it, "Good deeds in this life may lead to a happy rebirth in a better life."

This statue of Vishnu was carved in Punjab, in northern India, about a thousand years ago.

Buddhism

The second great religion born in India was Buddhism, which emerged between about 500 and 450 BCE. Buddhism kept some Vedic ideas such as karma, while offering a few new religious ideas. Those new concepts were primarily concerned with how people might discover life's truths and liberate the soul.

The early Buddhists were followers of a man who came to be called the Buddha, meaning "the enlightened one." To this day, no one knows the exact details of his life. Some aspects of his story may be factual, while others are probably legendary. What is certain is that the Buddha developed a new way of looking at humans and their daily struggles. Remarkably, the insights of a single person influenced hundreds of millions of people.

Monks pray at Bodh Gaya, where the Buddha is said to have attained enlightenment.

Buddha's Story

The man who became known as the Buddha was born Siddhartha Gautama in about 500 BCE. According to tradition, Siddhartha was a prince in a wealthy kingdom in northern India. As a youth, he enjoyed a life of comfort and knew nothing about what life was like for most people outside his father's palace. This changed when the prince was twenty-nine. He decided to leave the palace and observe everyday life in nearby villages. For the first time, he saw disease, suffering, and death, realities that shocked and saddened him.

Siddhartha was so affected by what he had seen that he gave up his privileged life. He adopted a life of poverty, self-denial, and extreme discipline. He sat alone for long periods, meditating, hoping to understand the true purpose of life.

One day, he had a sudden burst of insight. He realized that human existence is governed by four fundamental truths. First, life is filled with suffering or frustration; second, suffering results from greed, conceit, and sinful behavior; third, these problems can be overcome; and fourth, people can defeat the causes of suffering by put-

ting themselves on a path by which they transform themselves.

Having realized these truths, Siddhartha had attained enlightenment and from then on was called the Buddha. He preached about how others might also become enlightened and attracted a group of followers. They carried on his work when he died. Buddhism grew steadily, and today hundreds of millions of people follow it.

Buddhist monks pray at Shey Monastery, a holy site in northern India.

Buddhism became both a philosophy and a religion. Buddhists do not recognize an all-powerful creator god. Instead, they advocate that each person should search for a path to finding wisdom, peace, and contentment. He or she can do this with the aid of priests, or the person can do it alone by following what the Buddha called the Eightfold Path.

The Eightfold Path

The Buddha's path to spiritual harmony consists of eight parts, each a behavior or trait to be mastered. The eight parts are often depicted as a wheel. The first is right views, or understanding. The second is right goals, or purpose. The other six are right speech; right behavior or actions; right occupation or livelihood; right effort; right thoughts; and right concentration, or meditation.

The Buddha also preached that people should not kill any living thing. Neither should they steal, lie, or get drunk. Someone who follows such good actions, he said, can get closer to a state of peace, harmony, and happiness called nirvana.

After the Buddha's death in the late 400s BCE, Buddhist ideas were carried to other lands. In this way, the faith took root in China, Korea, Cambodia, Thailand, and Japan. Meanwhile, Indian Buddhists erected handsome temples across the country. These were maintained by priests and were quiet, clean places for the faithful to meditate and conduct rituals.

Jainism

The Buddha was not the only early Indian religious leader who sought a way to liberate the soul and find life's truths. About a century before the Buddha was preaching, another young Indian prince underwent a great spiritual transformation. His name was Vardhamana Mahavira, and the faith he established is called Jainism. Mahavira came to believe that all life is potentially divine, and that every bit of matter has a soul. That is, all forms of life—including mammals, fish, insects, and plants—have souls. It is a mistake and harmful, therefore, to kill any living thing, including plants. Like Hindus and Buddhists, Jains believe in karma. Untangling oneself from karma, according to Jainist belief, will liberate the soul and allow one to live without ignorance and suffering.

As in Buddhism, the path to enlightenment involves practicing self-discipline and good behavior. Jains take vows— some are very strict ones followed by Jain monks and some are

Ancient Temples

Thousands of Hindu and Buddhist temples were built in India in premodern times. They had various purposes. In Hinduism, the temples' main purpose was to serve as a home for a deity. Temples also inspired devotion in worshippers and provided them with quiet places to meditate.

Many of these structures are in an architectural form that first appeared more than two thousand years ago. Called stupas, they imitated the look of rounded mounds of earth in which families buried their dead. People constructed stupas from stone blocks, baked bricks, wood, plaster, and other materials. They decorated them, and over time some stupas became visually splendid and beautiful. Typical were brightly painted walls, finely crafted outside fences and gates, and, in the case of Hindu stupas, elaborate displays of statues of gods made of wood, stone, or metal.

One of the oldest and most impressive temples in India is the Mahabodhi Temple in Bihar, in the country's northeastern sector. The original structure was erected in about 250 BCE on what was believed to be the spot where the Buddha attained enlightenment. The temple rests atop a highly decorated 180-foot (55 m) brick tower, which was built more recently. Beside the temple is a tree planted from a seedling that tradition claims was taken from a cutting of the original Bodhi tree, the sacred fig tree under which the Buddha sat and meditated.

Two new Jain monks take the oath of austerity, in which they vow to live according to Jainism's strict rules.

less severe ones pledged by ordinary worshippers. The monks must always speak the truth, and they live apart from society and most people. Average Jains vow to be vegetarians and not take jobs that will involve the knowing destruction of life. A devout Jain cannot be a hunter or fisherman.

Sikhism

Another major religion, Sikhism, emerged in the fifteenth century in India. The teachings of ten Sikh gurus, or spiritual leaders, who lived between 1469 and 1708, form the basis of the religion. Unlike Hindus, Sikhs believe in a single god. Sikhs believe that God is present everywhere and can be seen by the spiritually enlightened.

Work, family, and service to others are important religious goals for Sikhs. Attitudes related to this world such as greed, pride, and anger keep people separated from God and prevent them from achieving enlightenment. Meditating on God and the message of God enables Sikhs to move toward enlightenment.

Equality is one of the most fundamental principles of Sikhism. Sikhs reject India's caste system that divides people into different classes. They are supposed to defend the rights of

A Sikh man prays before the Golden Temple in Amritsar, in northern India.

Indians light candles, lamps, and fireworks to celebrate Diwali, the festival of light.

all creatures. According to Sikh ideals, people should work for the good of others and share what they have, particularly food.

Religious Celebrations

Each religion practiced in India has yearly festivals and holidays. Over time, some of these rites have developed into major celebrations observed by a large part of the population. Diwali, Hinduism's most important annual festival, is a good example. Many non-Hindu Indians join in the festivities just as many non-Christian Americans celebrate Christmas. Diwali is celebrated for five days in late October or early November, and is called the festival of lights. This is because people across the land stage fireworks displays in honor of Lakshmi, the goddess of prosperity and companion to Vishnu, preserver of life. It is customary for Indians of all walks of life to pray for success and wealth during Diwali.

Major Religious Festivals

Festival	Time of Year	Celebrates
Lohri	January	End of winter
Holi	March	Arrival of spring
Buddha Purnima	May or June	Birth of Buddha
Raksha Bandhan	July or August	Brother-sister ties
Onam	September or October	End of monsoons
Ramlila	October	Killing of a demon
Diwali	October or November	Prosperity

Another widely observed religious holiday, Holi, is called the festival of color and carnival of riots. It takes place in early March, and it marks the coming of spring and honors Krishna and other deities. All over India, people light bonfires and play pranks on one another. Many run through the streets throwing colored water or powders at anyone close enough to douse.

People celebrating Holi often end up covered in colored powder.

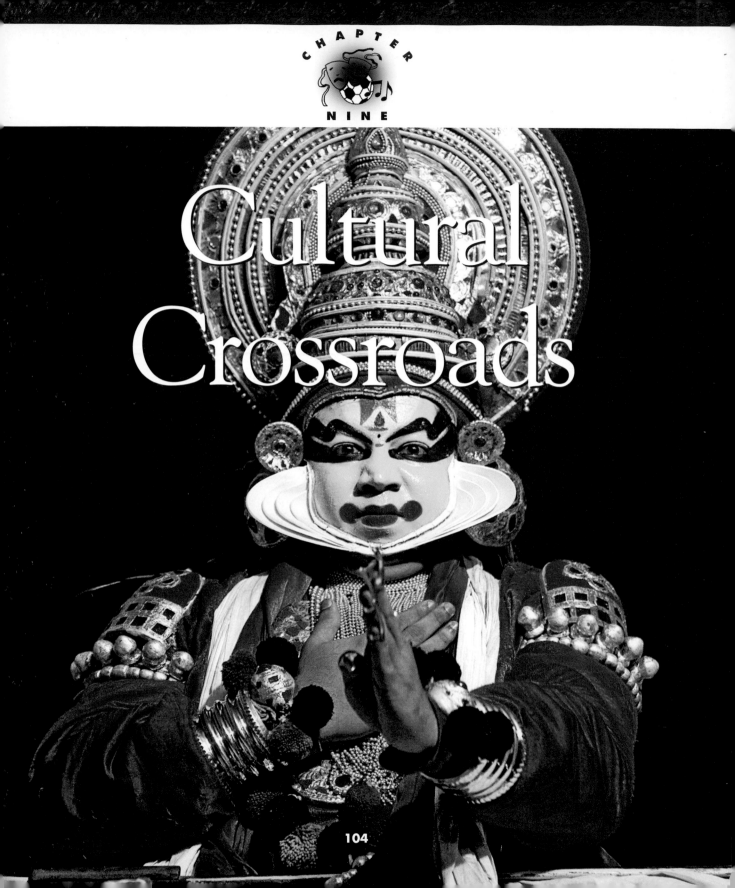

Cultural Crossroads

Indian's cultural and artistic heritage is amazingly diverse, expressive, and vibrant. Indians enjoy playing a wide array of sports. They love music, dancing, theater, and other performing arts. Literary traditions are strong in India. People of all walks of life cherish a collection of epics and other ancient written works. And Indians are as crazy about movies as Americans are. In fact, India's film industry is the world's largest, far surpassing that of the United States in sheer numbers of movies made each year.

Two broad and dissimilar cultural traditions run through most of India's popular culture and art. One consists of time-honored customs and practices. Many of these developed before the British arrived in the subcontinent. The other cultural tradition is made up of foreign customs and institutions, mostly British, that took strong root in the country during the years of the Raj. Most Indians did not want British rule and longed for independence. Yet many Indians came to admire British culture and customs, and adopted them to one degree

Opposite: **Kathakali, a form of classical Indian drama, features elaborate costumes and makeup.**

Boys play cricket in the streets of India.

or another. As a result, today, after more than six decades of independence, various aspects of Indian culture have a distinctly British flavor.

A Thirst for Sports

That British legacy is most obvious in the world of sports. Several of the country's most popular sports—including field hockey, tennis, and soccer—were introduced by the British. But the greatest example is cricket. Invented in England in the 1500s, cricket is the most beloved sport in India. Indeed, it is widely viewed as a national obsession. People of all ages and backgrounds play it in backyards, on school fields, or on professional teams. The best players are national celebrities.

Eyes are glued to televisions all across India when the national team plays. Regular foes include England, Australia, New Zealand, Sri Lanka, Bangladesh, Pakistan, and South Africa. In 2011, India won the coveted Cricket World Cup in a hard-fought battle against Sri Lanka.

Although tennis lacks the enormous fan following of cricket, it has been growing in popularity among Indians in recent decades. The sport enjoyed a major boost in 1999 when Leander Paes and Mahesh Bhupathi won the doubles title at Wimbledon, the world's most prestigious tennis tournament. In 2009, Bhupathi teamed up with Sania Mirza to capture the doubles title at the Australian Open.

India's Great Tennis Champ

One of the finest tennis players in the world, Mahesh Bhupathi was born in Chennai, India, in 1974. As a young man, he traveled to the United States and attended the University of Mississippi, where he became a star on the tennis team. Bhupathi turned pro in 1995. In the years that followed, he racked up four Grand Slam doubles titles and seven Grand Slam mixed doubles titles. (Grand Slam tournaments are the world's four top tennis tournaments.) In all, he won forty-eight tennis titles. In 2001, the Indian government awarded Bhupathi one of its highest honors. Known as the Padma Shri, it recognizes distinguished contributions made by Indians in cultural activities that include the arts, literature, education, and sports.

When India gained independence, field hockey was chosen as the national sport. Intense interest in the game was reflected by six Olympic gold medals won by Indian teams between 1928 and 1956. Two more Olympic wins came in 1964 and 1980. Over the years, however, the popularity of field hockey among Indians has declined, mostly because of the growing mania for cricket.

In spite of the popularity of cricket and other Western games in modern India, the country's thirst for athletic games includes several widely admired traditional Indian sports. One is *silambam*, a type of fencing or martial art in which each player tries to touch his opponent's body with a thin wooden staff. Another popular Indian martial art, *thoda*, combines expert archery with rapid leg kicks. One of the oldest and

An Ancient Sport

Kabaddi is a very ancient sport. Some evidence suggests that a form of it was played on the subcontinent as long ago as four thousand years. According to legend, the game originated during an incident in which a child hit a playmate and swiped his candy. The victim gave chase and returned the punch before running away himself. This pattern of attacking and running is the basis for kabaddi. Taking the offensive, one player attacks a team of seven others, attempting to make contact with each and thereby eliminating him or her from the game. Meanwhile, the constantly running and dodging defenders must try to keep the attacker from returning to his or her home side.

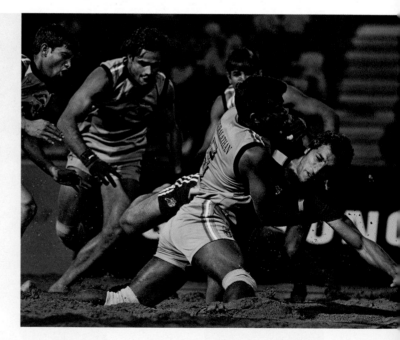

Dance is an important part of Indian culture. Here, women dance at a wedding celebration.

best-loved of Indian games is *kabaddi*, which features rough-and-tumble moves like those in rugby and wrestling.

Classical Indian Culture

Many of the same people who are passionate about sports also love traditional Indian music, arts, literature, and crafts. In particular, people all across the country take great pride in ancient, or classical, Indian culture. This is evident from the strong current of classical themes seen in everyday life. For example, ancient dances are performed at events such as weddings, parties celebrating a child's birth, and holiday festivals. Similarly, some of the most popular movies and TV shows are dramatizations of ancient classical literary works.

Classical Indian dancing originated as part of ancient religious ceremonies performed in temples. The art form combines beautifully coordinated hand movements, facial expressions, body postures, and dance steps. The visual effect is heightened by the stunning outfits worn by the dancers. Brightly colored skirts swirl as female dancers move. Flowers and jewelry adorn their hair, upper body, and wrists.

The traditional music that accompanies dance uses patterns called ragas. Some ragas date back many centuries, while others are modern compositions inspired by the ancient versions. These tunes are set to various lively rhythms known as talas. Among the more common instruments are drums, the guitarlike *rabab*, and an oboelike reed pipe called the *shehnai*.

The shehnai is made of wood and has a metal bell at the end. It typically has six to eight finger holes.

Indians have a great love for classical Indian literature. Particularly popular are the nation's two great epic poems—the Ramayana and the Mahabharata. The core stories emerged during the Vedic Age, possibly as early as 800 BCE, although they continued to evolve. The Ramayana describes the daring and gallant deeds of Rama, a prince who is also the god Vishnu in disguise. The Mahabharata is an enormous epic poem consisting of around one hundred thousand stanzas, making it several times longer than the Bible. It tells the story of a war fought between two giant armies, a battle for power between two parts of a family. Tragically, this battle leads to the family being destroyed.

India's two national epics are so revered that they continue to inspire other cultural forms. Musical pieces, dances, plays,

The Ramayana tells the story of Rama (the god Vishnu) and his bride, Sita. This painting shows their wedding procession.

A Splendid Arts Center

India's leading venue for classical Indian music and dancing is the National Center for the Performing Arts (NCPA) in Mumbai. This huge, beautifully decorated, state-of-the-art facility also showcases the works of other kinds of artists. It features five theaters, a photo gallery, a recording studio, and a library for research on the arts. One of the five theaters, the thousand-seat Tata Theater, regularly presents plays by the greatest Indian and international playwrights. Annual film festivals are also held in the theaters. In addition, the NCPA is home to the Symphony Orchestra of India, founded in 2006, which plays Western classical music. The top-notch musicians double as teachers who pass on their knowledge to Indian children.

sculptures, paintings, novels, comic books, TV shows, and movies have all depicted them. One of India's most widely watched TV shows was a dramatization of the Mahabharata. The ninety-four-episode series, directed by Ravi Chopra, originally ran from 1988 to 1990. Since then, it continues in reruns, not only in India but also in England and other countries. The Ramayana has been filmed multiple times, too, including in several animated versions.

Considering the enduring popularity of India's classical literature, it is not surprising that many modern Indian writers have been inspired by these ancient writings. Novelists, playwrights, and poets have also taken their ideas and characters

India's Greatest Writer

Universally recognized as India's greatest writer, Rabindranath Tagore (1861–1941) was also a painter, composer, and philosopher. He began writing in his teens and over time turned out numerous plays, poems, and novels. He also socialized and traveled with other great thinkers, including German scientist Albert Einstein and English writer H. G. Wells. In 1913, Tagore became the first non-European to win the Nobel Prize in Literature. He also wrote the text for India's national anthem. The following description of a dream is from Tagore's poetry collection *Thought Relics*.

Last night I dreamt that I was the same boy that I had been before my mother died. She sat in a room in a garden house on the bank of the Ganges. I carelessly *passed by without paying attention to her, when all of a sudden it flashed through my mind with an unutterable longing that my mother was there. At once I stopped and went back to her and bowing low touched her feet with my head. She held my hand, looked into my face, and said: "You have come!"*

Chetan Bhagat is the best-selling English-language novelist in India.

from Indian history and culture. The greatest early modern Indian writer was Rabindranath Tagore. He combined a fascination for India's past with deep concerns for its modern realities and problems.

A number of recent Indian writers have tackled India's problems in both serious and humorous ways, and gained large audiences. Chetan Bhagat attracted many young adult readers in India, England, and other countries with his 2004 novel *Five Point Someone*. It follows the misadventures of three young Indian men trying to learn engineering at one of the country's many technical schools. Aravind Adiga also struck literary gold with *The White Tiger*. It is a sober look at poverty and other social problems in modern India.

An array of colorful Indian film posters

Indian Cinema

Any discussion of modern Indian culture would be incomplete without a look at the unique cultural phenomenon known as Bollywood. A takeoff on the name Hollywood, the center of U.S. filmmaking, the term Bollywood is a slogan for India's huge film industry. The chief movie studio, Film City, is in Mumbai. It shoots films mostly in Hindi. Smaller but very active studios that make movies in Tamil and Bengali are located in Chennai and Kolkata.

Together, these studios turn out more than eight hundred films annually. That is more than twice the output of U.S. filmmakers. An estimated fourteen million people pack the country's movie theaters every day.

Most Indian films follow a formula that has come to be called masala, a word meaning "mixed spice." This is because the average film combines romance, action, and comedy with periodic scenes of characters singing and dancing. Though the films often address social issues, everything works out for the better at the end of the typical Bollywood movie. For this reason, some viewers, both inside and outside India, have complained that these films ignore most of life's problems. One prominent Indian movie producer answered this charge by saying, "It's called escapist cinema. Why should somebody pay to see a film with poverty in it when they see poverty in their neighborhood every day?"

Aishwarya Rai Bachchan is one of the most popular Bollywood actresses. She has appeared in more than forty films.

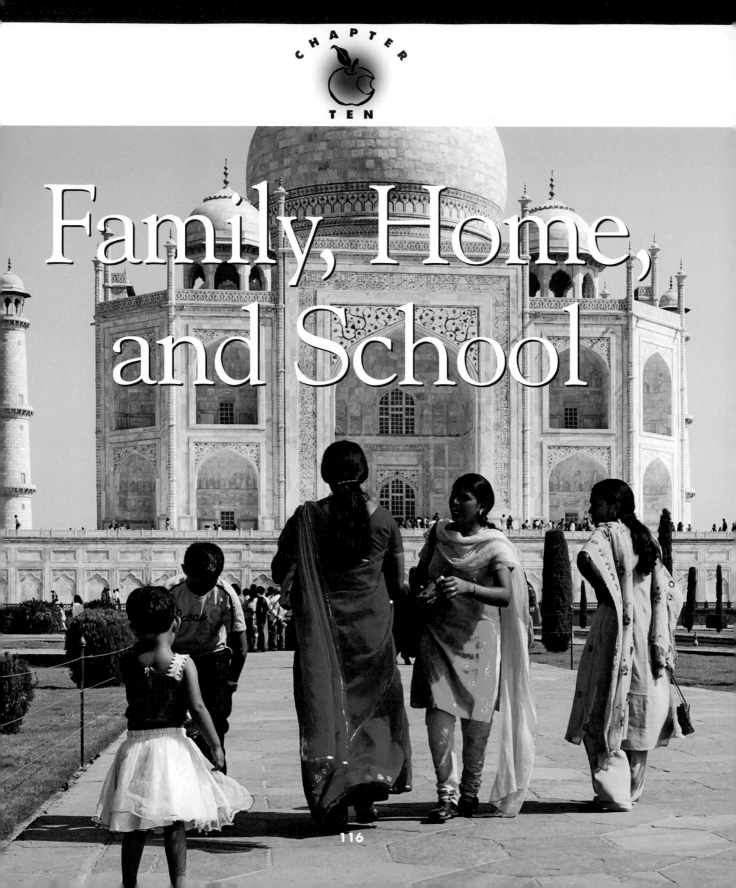

Family, Home, and School

I N SOME WAYS, FAMILY LIFE IN INDIA IS SIMILAR TO that in Western countries such as the United States and Canada. Indian parents love their children dearly and want to protect them and give them the best lives possible. Indian children love and respect their parents, and for the most part follow their rules.

But the customs of Indian families differ in a number of ways from those of their Western counterparts. First, many Indians live in extended families, which might include aunts, uncles, cousins, grandparents, and other relatives. Ten to fifteen or more people often live under the same roof in India. By Western standards, this is both crowded and lacking in privacy, but Indians see it as natural. In fact, most Indian children readily accept sharing a bedroom with siblings or other family members. They view the Western ideal of each child having his or her own bedroom as odd.

Opposite: **A family walks toward the Taj Mahal in Agra.**

Family and Marriage

Another way that Indian home life differs is in its rigid, formal structure. There is an accepted ladder of authority that each family member is expected to respect. With rare exceptions, the father is seen as the head of the household. No matter how old the children are, if they live in his house, they are expected to ask his permission to go out. By custom, his wife or the oldest married woman living in the home has the right to control the behavior of all other female relatives. The wife normally asks her husband his opinion or permission in all important family matters. Also, when others are present, she

On average, women in India have 2.6 children.

refrains from saying his name aloud, instead getting his attention by saying "excuse me," "hello," or "my husband."

Strict rules govern the performance of household duties as well. Women are expected to do the cooking and cleaning. If relatives or friends are visiting, the females among them pitch in to help the mother and her daughters. Male visitors are exempt from such chores. In middle-class and well-to-do homes, most of the household duties are done by servants. In many cases, these helpers—who come from the poorer social classes—live with the family, sometimes for many years or even generations.

Still another family custom rarely seen in the West but common in India is arranged marriages. Some young adult Indians choose their own mates. Although this approach is becoming more acceptable, it remains uncommon. In most Indian families, the parents choose their children's life mates.

School Time

When they are not at home with their families, many Indian children are at school. In fact, children in India attend school for about eleven months each year.

Like Western countries, India has both primary (elementary) schools and secondary schools, which are for junior high and high school students. Enrollment for these two kinds of schools has long been, and continues to be, uneven. The United Nations reports that in 2009, 91 percent of Indian boys and 88 percent of Indian girls enrolled in the country's primary schools. However, in the same year, only 61 percent of boys and 52 percent of girls registered to attend secondary

Indian Weddings

Marriage celebrations are among the most important of the family customs and rituals in India. The typical Indian wedding is a large, formal, and joyous affair. Indeed, it is not unusual for up to a thousand guests to attend a wedding. So those who plan and pay for these celebrations—usually the bride's parents—often incur debts that take several years to repay. Generally, they see this as a worthwhile expense because an impressive wedding display improves their social status.

A majority of Indian weddings follow Hindu customs. If money and other factors permit, the groom sits on a colorfully decorated horse or some other form of transportation that symbolizes his high status. Elephants are popular, as are buggies or decorated cars. Accompanied by siblings, cousins, other male relatives, friends, musicians, and dancers, he rides to the site of the ceremony. There, the bride's family greets him, and there is a fireworks display. As the actual ceremony begins, the groom and bride ask or wish for good health, spiritual peace, healthy children, and a long life together. Then the bride's father places her right hand in the groom's right hand, and the bride's mother pours water on the couple's palms. Afterward, the families and guests feast, dance, and play games.

schools. The main reason for this gap in school attendance is poverty. Because so many Indians are poor or nearly so, parents often need their children to take full-time jobs to help support the family.

Those young people who do attend secondary school study a wide range of subjects. Usually, a group of forty or fifty students remains in one classroom for the whole school day. Every forty minutes, a different teacher arrives to cover a specific subject. Those subjects include math, science, modern history, India's government and constitution, art, and various Indian and foreign languages. All schools have student clubs in areas such as music, dancing, and drama.

In the Home

The average Indian Hindu home has a small shrine or altar at which the family worships and meditates. Displayed atop the altar are one or more *murti*, images of the gods. The usual

Major National Holidays

Republic Day	January 26
Independence Day	August 15
Gandhi's Birthday	October 2
Christmas	December 25

Some major holidays are based on the lunar calendar, which follows the phases of the moon. The dates shift from year to year on the Western calendar. These holidays include:
Prophet Muhammad's Birthday
Holi
Ram Navami (honors Rama)
Buddha Purnima
Diwali

The Caste System

One factor that helps to determine the number of Indian children enrolled in schools is the country's caste system. The castes are like social classes. They roughly correspond to upper class, upper middle class, middle class, and lower class in terms of general social position and social prospects. Below the lower class is a fifth group, the untouchables, who make up about 15 percent of the population. They are very poor and traditionally do jobs seen as dirty, such as garbage collection. The government has passed laws making it illegal to discriminate according to caste. But such prejudice and unfair treatment still exist in some quarters, especially against the untouchables. Because of their poverty and low social rank, most untouchable children never attend school, which makes it extremely difficult for them to ever improve their status.

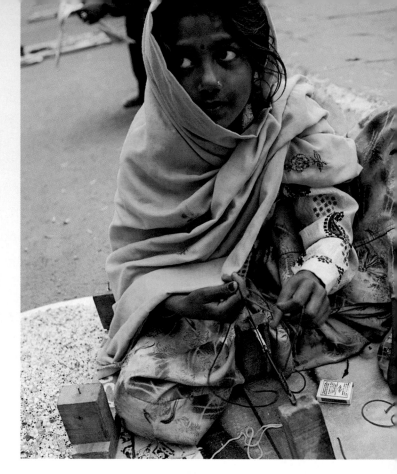

custom is to light a lamp, which symbolizes the god's presence in the room. The lamp is often waved before the deity as an offering of light. A bell is rung as an offering of sound. The worshippers then pay their respects by offering the god water, food, or flowers.

The average Indian kitchen is quite different from kitchens in the United States and Canada. It is rare for Indian kitchens to have either hot water or an electric dishwasher. Instead, dirty dishes are cleaned under cold running water. Also, most Indians cook their food on portable ranges similar to camping stoves. These are usually powered by bottled natural gas, although the more expensive homes have piped

gas. Ovens are also rare because most Indian cooking does not involve baking or broiling. Most Indian kitchens have few or no cupboards, though they often have shelves, and it is customary to hang pots, pans, and utensils from wall hooks.

Pots and utensils hang from the wall in this kitchen in New Delhi.

Life's Path in a Game

Both at school and at home, Indian children play games, including physical ones and board games. Perhaps the most popular board game is *Moksha Patam*, or Snakes and Ladders (called Chutes and Ladders in some countries). The game illustrates the role of karma in life. The path a player takes from the board's lower part to its upper part represents a person's path in life. That path can be aided by good deeds (symbolized by the ladders) or hindered by bad deeds (symbolized by the snakes). A typical board is divided into 64, 100, or 144 squares, and the object is to navigate the squares and reach the top row. Dice throws determine how many squares a player moves. Landing on a square containing the lower section of a ladder allows a player to move upward to the square containing that ladder's upper section. Similarly, landing on a square with a snake forces the player to move downward.

Eating in India

The meals prepared in Indian kitchens are diverse and tasty. Most Indians eat breakfast early—between 6:00 and 7:00 a.m. Breakfast tends to be a light meal. The fare, which varies from one region of the country to another, can include steamed rice cakes and lentils, fried biscuits, or rice pancakes. Lunch is often between 1:00 and 2:00 p.m. and usually consists of some sort of rice dish or bread, a vegetable dish, and perhaps also a meat dish. After lunch, during the hot part of the day, people take a rest. Dinner or supper is often less elaborate and can involve leftovers from lunch. Dinner is served late in India, often between 8:00 and 8:30 p.m.

Pakoras are a popular snack. They are breaded, deep-fried vegetables.

Dishes often include combinations of vegetables, lentils, rice, bread, and yogurt. Although most Indians are vegetarians, an increasing percentage of the population likes meat. But for most of them, "meat" means chicken, fish, mutton, or eggs. Some meats common in other countries are avoided in India. Devout Hindus and Sikhs do not eat beef, and Muslims refrain from pork. Dessert can be fruit, rice pudding, ice cream, or carrot halva. Another popular dessert is *faluda*, sweet noodles flavored with saffron and rose water.

Rice, bread, and vegetables are all common at Indian meals.

Indian food is now popular around the world. Many people love the complex spice combinations that might include cinnamon, garlic, turmeric, cumin, coriander, ginger, saffron, and many, many more. Many Indian dishes are extremely spicy, so spicy in fact that many people who did not grow up with them cannot tolerate them.

Different parts of India have very different typical foods. These vary based upon what vegetables and fruits grow in a region, whether most people there are vegetarian, and the influences of newcomers who migrated there. Goa, on the western coast, has a cuisine based on seafood. But in Gujarat, a state not far to the north of Goa, most of the food is vegetarian. There, people often produce dishes that are both sweet and spicy. Like so much about India, the food is extremely diverse.

A woman sells spices at a market in Goa. Many different spices are used in Indian cooking.

Carrot Halva

This popular, nutritious, and delicious dessert is often made in winter, when carrots ripen.

Ingredients

1 cup carrots, grated coarsely

¾ cup sugar

2½ cups milk

Cardamom seeds

½ cup ghee (butter cooked
    until the water evaporates and
    milk solids have separated out)

Cashew nuts

Directions

Combine the carrots with the sugar and milk and cook at low heat until the mixture becomes thick. Add the ghee, some cardamom seeds, and a few cashew nuts. Stir until the mixture becomes thick again. Spread the mixture onto a greased tray and allow it to cool for about thirty minutes. Cut the carrot halva into squares and serve.

Timeline

Indian History

Small farms exist in northwestern India's Indus Valley.	ca. 4000 BCE
Harappan civilization begins to decline.	ca. 1900 BCE
Aryans migrate into India; India's Vedic Age begins.	ca. 1500 BCE
Darius I of Persia's Achaemenian Empire invades western India.	ca. 515 BCE
Siddhartha Gautama, called the Buddha, begins preaching the doctrines of Buddhism.	500s BCE
The Macedonian Greek conqueror Alexander the Great invades western India.	326 BCE
Chandragupta Maurya founds the Mauryan Dynasty in northern India.	321 BCE
The last Mauryan king falls from power.	184 BCE
The Gupta Empire is established.	300s CE
The Huns invade India.	400s
A Muslim kingdom called the Delhi Sultanate is established in northern India.	1206
The Timurids, led by Babur, invade northern India and establish the Mughal Empire.	1526

World History

ca. 2500 BCE	Egyptians build the pyramids and the Sphinx in Giza.
ca. 563 BCE	The Buddha is born in India.
313 CE	The Roman emperor Constantine legalizes Christianity.
610	The Prophet Muhammad begins preaching a new religion called Islam.
1054	The Eastern (Orthodox) and Western (Roman Catholic) Churches break apart.
1095	The Crusades begin.
1215	King John seals the Magna Carta.
1300s	The Renaissance begins in Italy.
1347	The plague sweeps through Europe.
1453	Ottoman Turks capture Constantinople, conquering the Byzantine Empire.
1492	Columbus arrives in North America.
1500s	Reformers break away from the Catholic Church, and Protestantism is born.

Indian History

The Taj Mahal is completed by Mughal ruler Shah Jahan.	1643
A major rebellion called the Sepoy Mutiny erupts against the British in northern India.	1857
The Indian National Congress is formed to work toward Indian independence.	1885
Mohandas Gandhi begins leading nonviolent protests against the British.	1920s
Archaeologists begin excavations of Harappan ruins at Harappa.	1921
India gains independence from Britain; India is partitioned into two nations, India and Pakistan.	1947
India's first prime minister, Jawaharlal Nehru, dies.	1964
The Green Revolution allows India to increase its agricultural output.	1970s
India announces it has nuclear weapons.	1974
India fights its fourth war against neighboring Pakistan.	1999
India's population reaches 1.2 billion.	2011

World History

1776	The U.S. Declaration of Independence is signed.
1789	The French Revolution begins.
1865	The American Civil War ends.
1879	The first practical lightbulb is invented.
1914	World War I begins.
1917	The Bolshevik Revolution brings communism to Russia.
1929	A worldwide economic depression begins.
1939	World War II begins.
1945	World War II ends.
1957	The Vietnam War begins.
1969	Humans land on the Moon.
1975	The Vietnam War ends.
1989	The Berlin Wall is torn down as communism crumbles in Eastern Europe.
1991	The Soviet Union breaks into separate states.
2001	Terrorists attack the World Trade Center in New York City and the Pentagon near Washington, D.C.
2004	A tsunami in the Indian Ocean destroys coastlines in Africa, India, and Southeast Asia.
2008	The United States elects its first African American president.

Fast Facts

Official name: Republic of India

Capital: New Delhi

Official language: Hindi

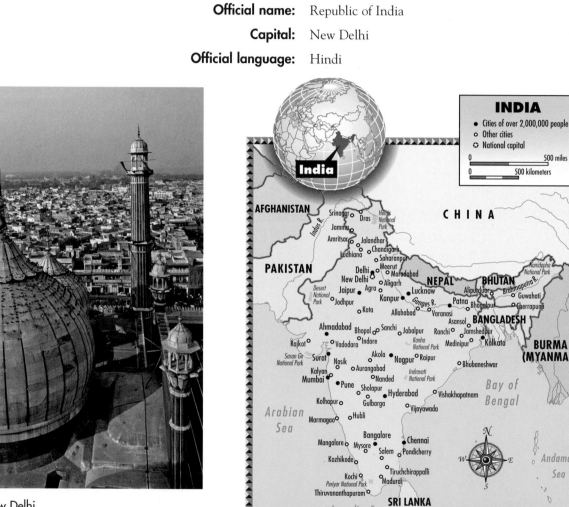

New Delhi

Indian flag

Official religion:	None
Year of founding:	1947
Government:	Parliamentary democracy
National anthem:	"*Jana Gana Mana*"
Chief of state:	President
Head of government:	Prime minister
Area:	1,298,800 square miles (3,364,000 sq km)
Coordinates of geographic center:	20°00' N, 77°00' E
Bordering countries:	Burma (or Myanmar) and Bangladesh to the east; Nepal and Bhutan to the northeast; China to the north; and Pakistan to the west
Highest elevation:	Mount Kanchenjunga, 28,201 feet (8,596 m) above sea level
Lowest elevation:	Indian Ocean, sea level
Average annual rainfall:	47 inches (120 cm)
Longest river:	Ganges, 1,565 miles (2,519 km)
Largest glacier:	Siachen, 1.7 by 47 miles (2.7 by 75.6 km)
Largest lake:	Chilka, about 450 square miles (1,165 sq km) during the wettest season
National population (2011 est.):	1.2 billion

Western Ghats

Taj Mahal

Currency

Population of major cities (with suburbs, 2011 est.):

Delhi	21,700,000
Mumbai	19,700,000
Kolkata	15,300,000
Chennai	7,400,000
Bangalore	7,100,000

Landmarks:

▶ *Gateway of India,* Mumbai

▶ *Indian Museum,* Kolkata

▶ *Jaipur House,* New Delhi

▶ *Mahabodhi Temple,* Bihar

▶ *Taj Mahal,* Agra

Economy: India has a diverse and thriving economy, the fifth largest in the world in 2010. It mines iron ore, bauxite, coal, copper, and dozens of other minerals and metals, and uses them to manufacture a wide range of products, including steel, cars, electrical equipment, cement, and computer software. Textile manufacturing is also an important industry. India is the world's largest exporter of rubber. Its major agricultural products are rice, wheat, and coarse grains. Service industries such as information technology, telecommunications, and banking are also important to the Indian economy.

Currency: The rupee. In 2011, 46 rupees equaled one U.S. dollar.

System of weights and measures: Metric system

Literacy rate: 61%

Fabric manufacturing plant

Jawaharlal Nehru

Common Hindi words and phrases:

haan	yes
na	no
dhanyavad	thank you
kripaya	please
kshama karen	excuse me/sorry
namasté	hello/good-bye
Aap kaisé hain?	How are you?
Mera naam . . .	My name is . . .

Prominent Indians:

Ashoka (ca. 300–232 BCE)
King and religious leader

Zahir-ud-Din Muhammad Babur (1483–1530)
Military general and ruler

Mahesh Bhupathi (1974–)
Tennis player

Ravi Chopra (1946–)
Film director

Indira Gandhi (1917–1984)
Prime minister

Mohandas Gandhi (1869–1948)
Political activist

Siddhartha Gautama (the Buddha) (ca. 500–late 400s BCE)
Religious leader

Jawaharlal Nehru (1889–1964)
Prime minister

Rabindranath Tagore (1861–1941)
Writer, painter, and composer

To Find Out More

Books

▶ Apte, Sunita. *India*. New York: Children's Press, 2009.

▶ Auboyer, Jeannine. *Daily Life in Ancient India*. London: Phoenix, 2002.

▶ Dalal, Anita. *Ancient India*. Des Moines, IA: National Geographic Children's Books, 2007.

▶ Heydlauff, Lisa. *Going to School in India*. Watertown, MA: Charlesbridge, 2005.

▶ Kalman, Bobbie. *India: The Land*. New York: Crabtree, 2010.

▶ Powell, Jillian. *Looking at India*. New York: Gareth Stevens, 2007.

▶ Schomp, Virginia. *Ancient India*. New York: Franklin Watts, 2005.

▶ Shores, Lori. *Teens in India*. Minneapolis: Compass Point Books, 2007.

DVDs

▶ *Gandhi*. Columbia-Tristar, 1982. *An Oscar-winning film about the great Indian thinker and political activist.*

▶ *The Story of India*. BBC-TV, 2009. *A six-part documentary about Indian history and culture.*

Web Sites

▶ **CIA World Factbook: India**
www.cia.gov/library/publications
/the-world-factbook/geos/in.html
*This large list of statistics and facts
about India is collected by the U.S.
government and updated annually.*

▶ **Internet Sacred Text Archive—
The Writings of Rabindranath
Tagore**
www.sacred-texts.com/hin
/tagore/index.htm
*To read some of the works by one of
the greatest Indian writers.*

▶ **National Portal of India**
http://india.gov.in
*For huge amounts of information and
links about Indian government, culture, and much more.*

▶ **UNICEF: India**
www.unicef.org/infobycountry
/india_statistics.html
*For statistics about modern Indian
society.*

Organizations and Embassies

▶ **Embassy of India**
2107 Massachusetts Avenue, NW
Washington, DC 20008
202/939-7000
www.indianembassy.org

▶ **High Commission of India**
10 Springfield Road
Ottawa, Ontario, Canada
K1M 1C9
613/744-3751
www.hciottawa.ca

▶ **Permanent Mission of India to
the United Nations**
235 East 43rd Street
New York, NY 10017
212/490-9660
www.un.int/india

▶ **Visit this Scholastic Web site for more information on India:**
www.factsfornow.scholastic.com

Index

Page numbers in *italics* indicate illustrations.

Meet the Author

A MEMBER OF THE ASSOCIATION OF ANCIENT HISTORIANS AND AN award-winning writer, Don Nardo specializes in writing about ancient civilizations, especially the histories and cultures of the Greeks, Romans, and other Mediterranean peoples. He has traveled widely in Europe and studied firsthand many of the ancient sites

he writes about. He has also written a volume on the history of ancient India, as well as discussed early India's connections with Europe and the Middle East in several of his books.

"I've always had a strong interest in India, including the exploits of the great modern leader Gandhi," he says. "So I immediately said yes when the editors of Scholastic's Enchantment of the World series asked me to do this general study of India. I began my research by reviewing the book I'd already written about ancient India and checking the main authoritative sources on that topic to see if any important new discover-

ies about ancient India had been made recently. I also collected and surveyed a number of books on modern Indian history, along with texts about India's geography, culture, and so forth. I found that travel guides and Internet Web sites were also quite helpful. Among the Web sites that provide up-to-date statistics on India, the one posted by the CIA (which maintains statistics for every country) is particularly good."

Nardo grew up in Massachusetts. He studied theater at Syracuse University and made his living for some years as an actor before returning to college to get his history degree. (One of his most memorable roles as an actor was the lead character in Indian writer Rabindranath Tagore's moving play *Sacrifice*.) In the 1980s, Nardo was asked to write some history books for young adults. Finding few accurate, well-written history texts, especially about ancient history, he continued writing books for students ranging from grade school to college level. In all, he has written more than 380 volumes of nonfiction, two novels, and several screenplays and teleplays, including works for Warner Bros. and ABC TV. Nardo resides with his wife, Christine, in Massachusetts.

Don Nardo as the royal priest in Tagore's play *Sacrifice*.

Photo Credits

Photographs © 2012:

age fotostock: 14, 57, 97 top (Dinodia Photos), 104 (Eduardo Grund), 122 (Marco Cristofori), 110 (Shehab Uddin), 52 top (The British Library), 47 (The Print Collector), 49 (Yogesh S. More);

Alamy Images: 18 (Angelo Hornak), 22 (Anne-Marie Palmer), 68 right, 130 left (Arco Images GmbH), 35, 36, 71, 93 (Dinodia Photos), 90 (Gavin Hellier), 85 (Graham Crouch), 8 (Images & Stories), 7 top, 86 (Jan Halaska), 2 (Jim Zuckerman), 20 bottom (John T.L), 33 (Jonathan Hewitt), 116 (Julian Claxton), 26 (Martin Harvey), 21, 109, 124 (Pep Roig), 127 (Profimedia International s.r.o.), 123 (Ruby), 114 (Sabena Jane Blackbird), 68 left (Stuart Forster India), 82 (Tim Gainey), 39 (Travel India);

AP Images: 113 (Ajit Solanki), 73 bottom (Anupam Nath), 58 (Desfors), 10 (Gautam Singh), 78 (Gurinder Osan), 60 (Manish Swarup), 59 (MB), 15 (Rajesh Kumar Singh), 56, 66;

Art Resource/Digital Image © 2012 Museum Associates/LACMA: 92 ;

Bridgeman Art Library/Ron Embleton/ Private Collection/© Look and Learn: 42;

Corbis Images/Kapoor Baldev/Sygma: 61;

Dreamstime: 96 (Astroskeptic), 23 (Digitalfestival), 95 (Kaetana), 19 (Nikmd), 97 bottom (Rangzen);

Getty Images: 24 (Abhijit Bhatlekar/ Bloomberg), 29 (Boris Breuer), 48 (Folco Quilici/Fratelli Alinari/Alinari Archives), 107 (Glyn Kirk/AFP), 77 top (Kainaz Amaria/Bloomberg), 108 (Mark Kolbe), 44 (Martin Gray/National Geographic), 102 (Narinder Nanu/AFP), 77 bottom, 100 (Noah Seelam/AFP), 103 (Poras Chaudhary), 80 (Sam Panthanky/ AFP), 88 (Stanley Breeden/National Geographic), 32 (Steve Winter/National Geographic), 67, 133 bottom (Wolf Suschitzky/Pix Inc./Time & Life Pictures);

Landov: 70 (B Mathur/Reuters), 121 (Krishna Murari Kishan/Reuters), 115 (Vincent Kessler/Reuters);

Media Bakery: back cover (Dallas/John Heaton), cover, 6 (Hemant Mehta), 74, 133 top (Philippe Michel), 62, 125;

Shutterstock, Inc.: 119 (De Visu), 99 (Image Focus), 76, 132 bottom (indianstockimages), 64, 131 top (Kevin George), 53, 132 top (nrg123), 7 bottom, 30 (palko72), 28 (sjgh), 13 (Vishal Shah);

Superstock, Inc.: 16, 34, 131 bottom (Eye Ubiquitous), 101 (Hemis.fr), 54 (Image Asset Management Ltd.), 118 (imagebroker.net), 52 bottom (Marka), 31 (NHPA), 12, 40, 50, 106 (Robert Harding Picture Library), 126 (Steve Vidler), 94 (Tomas Abad/age fotostock);

The Granger Collection: 41, 111;

The Image Works: 112 (Albert Harlingue/ Roger-Viollet), 46 (Mary Evans Picture Library), 55 (Roger-Viollet);

The Picture Desk/The Art Archive: 38.

Maps by XNR Productions, Inc.